Like
the First
Morning

"Replete with the wisdom of the saints and Christian writers through the centuries, together with his own experience of discipleship, Michael J. Ortiz, in this important new book, takes the reader through every aspect of the Morning Offering. Once you've read it, you'll never want to begin another day without pausing for a moment to offer your day, through this beautiful and powerful prayer, to God."

Most Rev. William E. Lori
Archbishop of Baltimore

"*Like the First Morning* shows why and how the Mass continues in our daily lives. Using literary, philosophical, and theological references, Michael Ortiz reflects on the Morning Offering prayer, giving it freshness and depth. Thus, he helps us not only to say the words of this traditional prayer, but to pray them as well."

Rev. James Kubicki, S.J.
National Director
Apostleship of Prayer

"For twelve years in Catholic school, I said the Morning Offering at the start of each day. Like all great Catholic prayers, it had the power of focusing the imagination—in this case on the extraordinary but finite gift of time. It reminded me not to waste a single day that God gave me. Of course, I never lived up to the sublime vision offered by this prayer, but saying it again each morning gradually developed something inside me that has helped guide my conscience for the rest of my life."

Dana Gioia
Poet and Former Chairman of the National Endowment of the Arts
(2003–2009)

"Once you read *Like the First Morning*, you'll reach for that instead of your first cup of coffee in the morning. With wisdom from saints and other notable Catholic authors, Michael Ortiz has devised a remarkable handbook for starting every morning out right—in the heart of our Lord and his Blessed Mother. This book is a must-have."

Marge Fenelon
Author of *Imitating Mary*

"Christian tradition has long urged that we set aside some time each day in which we direct ourselves to God. How we do this will vary widely, but a 'morning offering' has frequently been recommended. The Divine Office itself provides for this morning prayer. Michael Ortiz's short book is a welcome guide and model reflection on the various ways we can approach God. We are always helped by those who have written before us, the saints, the popes, and classical authors. There will always be good guides, but finding them is not always easy. *Like the First Morning* provides a refreshing approach for seeing the world 'as in the first morning,' to recall the account of Creation in Genesis. Each day becomes a renewal of all we know and are given, of what we can hope for."

Rev. James V. Schall, S.J.
Professor Emeritus
Georgetown University

"Michael Ortiz has written a beautiful book filled with the wisdom of Sacred Scripture, the world of nature, and literature about a simple Christian habit that is the Morning Offering. This work focuses on the very meaning of our lives—the glory of the Lord. A must read for all Christians devoted to giving their day and lives to God."

Rev. C. John McCloskey, III, S.T.D.
Research Fellow
Faith and Reason Institute
Washington, DC

"The Morning Offering has transformed my own life; Ortiz's insights renew my beloved daily devotion. From beginning to end, this book reads like a prayer. The practical suggestions at the end of each chapter encourage readers to join in the prayer, united in the love of Christ."

Grace Mazza Urbanski
Children's Ministry Director
Apostleship of Prayer

The Morning Offering
as a Daily Renewal

Like
the First

*M*orning

Michael J. Ortiz

AVE MARIA PRESS AVE Notre Dame, Indiana

Excerpt from "A Morning Prayer" by Eleanor Farjeon from *The Children's Bells,* published in 1967 by Faber and Faber, Oxford University Press. Used with permission from David Higham Agency. All rights reserved.

Selections from Wendell Berry's *Leavings* (copyright © 2010) are reprinted by permission of Counterpoint. All rights reserved.

Unless otherwise noted, all Scripture passages are from the *Revised Standard Version: Catholic Edition* of the Bible, copyright © 1952 and 1965 by the Division of Christian Education of the National Council of Churches of Christ in the USA. All rights reserved.

Verses marked DR are from *The Holy Bible Douay-Rheims Version,* copyright 1899 by the John Murphy Company.

Verses marked MKJV are from the *Holy Bible, Modern King James Version,* copyright 1962–1998 by Jay P. Green, Sr. Used by permission of the copyright holder.

Founded in 1865, Ave Maria Press is a ministry of the United States Province of Holy Cross.

www.avemariapress.com

Paperback: ISBN-13 978-1-59471-591-4

E-book: ISBN-13 978-1-59471-592-1

Cover image © shutterstock.com

Cover and text design by Katherine Robinson.

Printed and bound in the United States of America.

Library of Congress Cataloging-in-Publication Data

Ortiz, Michael J.

Like the first morning : the morning offering as a daily renewal / Michael J. Ortiz.

pages cm

Includes bibliographical references.

ISBN 978-1-59471-591-4 -- ISBN 1-59471-591-2

1. Spiritual life--Catholic Church--Meditations. I. Title.

BX2350.3.O55 2015

248.4'82--dc23

2014043797

In Memoriam:

Reverend Ronald S. Gillis

(1941–2013)

✳

*M*orning has broken, like the first morning.
Blackbird has spoken, like the first bird.
Praise for the singing, praise for the morning,
Praise for them springing fresh from the Word.
—Eleanor Farjeon, "A Morning Prayer"

*M*orning Offering

O Jesus, through the Immaculate Heart of Mary,
I offer you my prayers, works, joys,
and sufferings of this day,
for all the intentions of your Sacred Heart,
in union with the Holy Sacrifice of the Mass
throughout the world,
in thanksgiving for your favors, and for reparation
for my sins;
for the intentions of all my friends and relatives,
and in particular for the intentions
of the Holy Father.
Amen.

ontents

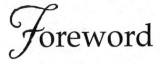

Foreword

"Anything we do, without offering it to God, is wasted."

This is how St. John Vianney succinctly and bracingly provides the "why" behind the practice of the Morning Offering.

Think about it. In the course of a given day, you or I can expect to encounter all kinds of people, situations, tasks, and surprises—both pleasant and unpleasant—together with a healthy dose of routine.

Yet for us who have been baptized, the living out of our daily lives is most definitely not a matter of just putting one foot in front of the other, and putting up with one thing after another, day after day, until the time allotted to us in this world is past. No! And that's where the Morning Offering comes in.

By means of this prayer, countless souls through the years have turned their daily "prayers, works, joys, and sufferings" into instances of praising God and obtaining graces for themselves, their families and friends, and even for people who are perhaps completely unknown to them.

It's interesting to note that the two patron saints of the missionary activity of the Church are St. Francis Xavier, who went to the ends of the earth to bring the Gospel to those who had never heard of Christ, together with St. Thérèse of the Child Jesus, who, once she had entered the Carmelite monastery in Lisieux, France, never left it. And yet St. Thérèse is today the copatron of the missions throughout the world.

She herself explains how this can be: "If the Church was a body composed of different members, it couldn't lack the noblest of all; it must have a heart, and heart burning with love. And I realized," she said, "that this love was the true motive force that enabled the other members of the Church to act; if it ceased to function, the Apostles would forget to preach the Gospel; the Martyrs would refuse to shed their blood" (*CCC*, 826).

And there we have it. Though relatively few of us are called to the unique and irreplaceable vocation of the contemplative, monastic life, as St. Thérèse was, all of us are called to intentionally offer each aspect of our day, no matter how mundane or seemingly insignificant, to God, with love. How God will use that self-offering is known only to him, but we know that he will use it.

For instance, maybe the stomach bug I just came down with—as miserable as it is for the moment—when intentionally offered to God, can obtain the grace to bring some soul back to the Church and to the sacraments. Maybe the chores around the house that seem so unappealing to me, when done with a smile and done as well as I can—and offered to God—can win for some troubled situation the grace of reconciliation. Maybe the time spent in prayer, perhaps in the presence of the Blessed Sacrament, even though it may sometimes seem dry and completely unproductive, can move some person, on the other side of the world, to love God.

As remarkable as this sounds, it's true.

Replete with the wisdom of the saints and Christian writers through the centuries, together with his own experience of discipleship, Michael J. Ortiz, in this important new book, takes the reader through every aspect of the Morning Offering. Once you've read it, you'll never want to begin another day without pausing for a moment to offer your day, through this beautiful and powerful prayer, to God.

On a personal note, I was delighted to learn that this book would be dedicated to the memory of Father Ronald Gillis, whom I had the privilege of knowing well for many years. Truly the Holy Mass was the center of his life as a man and a priest. For him, everything flowed from the Mass and led back to it. Consequently, Father Gillis's love for Christ and for his Church imbued every aspect of his day, and his impact—or Christ's impact through him—on the lives of countless students, families, seminarians, and priests was astoundingly and immeasurably fruitful.

So please join me in discovering more deeply the treasure contained in this magnificent prayer, explained so beautifully in this book. The results won't be fully known on this side of eternity. But we can trust that, in God's good providence, even the smallest aspects of our daily lives, offered to God, can bring forth a harvest worthy of heaven.

Most Reverend William E. Lori
Archbishop of Baltimore
August 2014

$\mathcal{J}$ntroduction

I'll never forget the first time I saw the Milky Way. Some friends and I were hunting on a farm in central Pennsylvania. It was late October, in the mid-1990s. We took an after-dinner walk. The breezes coming off the mountains to the south and north of us were crisp as they carried the fragrances of fireplaces burning oak and hickory. Looking at the stars above us, I noticed a band of white, vapory cloud spiraling into the fathomless night. I asked one of my friends (a retired physicist) standing beside me what it was.

"What's that? That's the Milky Way. Hundreds and hundreds of billions of stars hung up there for your delight!" My friend's eyes conveyed wonder at the glorious sight and at my surprising ignorance. While I had spent many a day and night as a boy in woods and streams and such, until that night, I had never seen with my own eyes that magnificent vision of cosmic prodigality known as the Milky Way. It was something of a revelation. This reminded me of a simple truth: we need guides to point out what we can't or don't notice on our own, but once it's pointed out to us, we must look with our own eyes or risk seeing nothing at all.

Christianity is both doctrine and life. This is so because any real kind of life must always be based on truth. If we are to live in the truth, we must have a guide—but not just any guide. We need someone who will be both an external guide directing us to what we can't see for ourselves and living strength within us so each moment of our lives will be transformed in the depths of our soul. A compass isn't much good if you can't go where it's pointing.

Typically, we tend to discount the importance of a guide in the spiritual life. We can handle that ourselves, thank you very much. But here we touch on the heart of the Christian Faith: only Christ has seen the Father (Jn 1:18). That is, only in the incarnate Word is the inner life of God revealed to us. Only in Christ can we approach the Father through the gift of faith; and only through the sacramental life of the Church, particularly in the Eucharist, do we receive the grace we need to live out that faith every day.

So how do we find a way into the life that Christ offers each of us?

One way into this life of God is called the Morning Offering. This manner of living takes the doctrine of Christian Faith and brings its life-giving graces to every moment of our day. It brings us to a guide who is also the way. As Christ told us, he is the truth and also the way to that truth that is life (Jn 14:6).

This offering is similar in spirit to an insight I almost literally stumbled upon a few years ago. While undergoing a difficult time in my life—nothing catastrophic but challenging nonetheless—I was walking to my office after attending Mass and saw before me a tiny cross on the floor. I picked it up and held it in my palm; it was a crucifix that must have fallen off a rosary. That wasn't the only thing missing. The body of Christ had fallen off too. In a moment, I realized that in all my troubles I was carrying a cross but one without Christ. How ridiculous! When we do that, we set ourselves up for failure. For only in Christ's Cross is found the peace and grace and everlasting life we all seek.

The Morning Offering is a time-tested way to avoid doing what I was doing, allowing us to enter more deeply into the very reality that is Christ. But what is the Morning Offering? Let me explain by way of a pop music song that was a major hit in the 1970s, a decade not known for its spiritual depth, yet if we dig a little deeper, some surprises await us. Amidst the tie-dyes and bell-bottoms and craziness, God is present though we don't spare him a thought. But when we do think of him, and better yet yearn for him with a listening heart, his truth becomes as clear as birdsong on a spring morning.

Morning Has Broken: The Story

In 1931, Eleanor Farjeon, an English writer of children's fiction and poetry, wrote the lyrics to "Morning Has Broken" for the editor of an Anglican hymnbook. Forty-one years later, Cat Stevens hit the top of the US pop charts with his acoustic version of the song. In 1977, Stevens converted to Islam, changing his name to Yusuf Islam. For eighteen years, he refrained from writing any music, but in 1995, he returned to the studio, inspired by his humanitarian concerns and his Islamic faith. On his website, he writes, "You can argue with a philosopher, but you can't argue with a good song."[1]

While philosophers may chatter on about each other's ideas, beauty—delicate as a rose and stronger than any lie—speaks to us with a unique authority. Alexander Solzhenitsyn, in his Nobel lecture, claimed just this point, saying, "Works of art which have scooped up the truth and presented it to us as a living force—they take hold of us, compel us, and nobody ever, not even in ages to come, will appear to refute them."[2] Even a simple song is still art by definition and may lodge in our memories with unusual tenacity due to its striking, sometimes haunting lyrics. Why is this? The answer is a mystery deeply wedded to how we experience the world.

Yusuf's "Morning Has Broken" has sold millions of copies worldwide. Its lyrics express, in simple but vivid images, a pristine moment in the history of humanity, one that touches the heart, perhaps even stirring within us a hope for something lost before we were born. His version has also worked its way into a number of modern hymnals, Catholic and Protestant. While a bit informal for worship use, a piece that celebrates how everything began with the lightsome joy of praise has more going for it than most pop songs.

Credit goes to Cat Stevens for realizing that Farjeon's lyrics touch on profound realities of life. Stevens wasn't alone in that recognition: in 1951, five years after becoming a Roman Catholic, Farjeon was the first recipient of the biennial Hans Christian Anderson Award, the highest international recognition given to an author of children's books. A reviewer wrote in that same year of the "abounding yea-saying joy" found in her romances and poetry.[3]

Farjeon's song has been incorporated into the Divine Office, the daily prayer of the Church, said by all clerics, religious, and many laity. And for centuries, Catholics have begun their day with a Morning Offering in various forms, concluding, as most Christian prayers do, with an "Amen," perhaps the most "yea-saying" word of any language. As the prayer at the beginning of this book shows, the Morning Offering is in tune with the core doctrines and practices of Christianity: Christ himself often went off alone, early in the morning, precisely to pray.

Many Christians have discovered that beginning the day with such an offering of prayer can, in a real sense, renew our souls so that it is something like the first morning of creation, with all its potential for grace. The freshness of each morning hour comes, in this sense, not from nostalgia, but from promises made by God. Echoing St. Augustine, Pope Benedict XVI reminds us, "Though the world grows old, Christ is forever young."[4]

Each chapter of this book—as one can see by its heading—offers a short reflection on the key points of the Morning Offering. This prayer is meant for all walks of life: the office, the home, the classroom, the workshop, the artist's studio, the farm, the barracks, the restaurant, and the laboratory. The Morning Offering is an act of piety. It is also a path of life, a manner of living that is as old as humanity.

Our first parents were created and put in a garden so they could offer Eden itself back to God in loving obedience. They failed, choosing to believe a lie rather than God (Gn 3:24). Christ suffered in a garden before he died, putting the Father's will before his own, and rose at dawn from a tomb set in a garden (Jn 19:41). Law and love can now meet in the heart of each person who accepts this gift, given in the quiet of the day as the sun's early light was touching the world.

"The place of perfect repose and inner harmony," wrote A. Bartlett Giamatti in his study of Renaissance epics, "is always remembered as a garden."[5] While Farjeon does not specifically mention a garden, her imagery is consistent with a garden's peaceful enclosure, with that quiet harmony of the first morning of creation unfolding from the word spoken by the Father. This gratuitous gift of being is none other than the world itself. Such a gift prompts certain questions: Why did God create us? Why did God give us this world to live in? What was his purpose in ushering into existence this universe of billions of galaxies, countless stars, and endless light years of space?

Thomas Aquinas gives us an astounding answer to these questions in his *Summa Theologiae*: "It would seem most fitting that by visible things the invisible things of God should be made known; *for to this end was the whole world made*."[6]

This is an amazing statement: all that is, the entire cosmos, from a flower to a collapsing star, exists to make known the ground of all being, God. This means, logically, that all things—repeat, all things—speak of him. Though marred by sin, the world we live in is bathed in light that reveals its Creator: "For with thee is the fountain of life; in thy light we shall see light" (Ps 35:10, DR). This psalm is a witness to our having been made for truth. The shadows of our broken world abide only in this endless light.

Here we come to the highest purpose of the human person: adoration of the Lord God. Before we are knowers, builders, artists, traders, or caregivers, we are created to be *adorers*

of God's luminous majesty simply because he is infinitely
good, the source of all that is. When we discover this core
meaning of the Morning Offering and make it a permanent
part of our life, we fulfill the plan God has had for us from
all eternity.

Our world, broken by sin, will only truly be renewed
from within. Offering all we have and are to the Lord God is
an indispensable element in this renewal; it is why we were
created in the first place.

Alone among all the visible creation, we are meant to
behold—knowingly—God's goodness. In addition, "The
unique position of man in the universe," writes Alexander
Schmemann in *For the Life of the World*, "is that he alone is to
bless God for the food and the life that he receives from Him."[7]
To bless God means to thank him in an act of adoration and
gratitude. That new morning in the garden tomb brings back
this primordial purpose, though in a more intimate manner.
The Church itself is foreshadowed in the Song of Songs as a
garden, with an enclosed fountain (Sg 4:12). In this prophetic
image, the "north wind" of the Holy Spirit dispenses the fra-
grant graces of redemption to all men and women, who—by
virtue of their baptismal promises—are now invited to offer
the world back to God, fulfilling the end for which all things
exist.

By making a Morning Offering, we renew the wonder
and promise of the morning of the Resurrection. The Sabbath is now that first day of the week, the *dies Dominicus*, or
the Lord's Day, emblem of the rebirth of the world by grace.
All things regain their voice. To the pure of heart, the whole
world sings of God.

Though the whole of creation gives glory to God, it is
in need of the redemption that comes only through the Cross
of Christ. Because of that, the sacrifice of the Mass provides
the focal point of our day. I remember well the advice of a
holy priest—to whom this book is dedicated—who was for
decades a chaplain at two private schools. In his homilies, he

would frequently say, "When I raise the paten at the offertory, I want you to make it really heavy with all your intentions. Pile onto it all your books, and all the burdens of your study, your hopes for yourself and for your family, for the Church, just pile them all very high, and then with your prayers, help me bring them to God." How simple and yet how excellent an understanding this is of the Mass as an action, a sacrifice, and a ritual designed by God to take us to God.

Though Shakespeare could evoke the language of despair, he also saw the world as the gift it is, especially in the resolution of his dramas in their final scene. For instance, in the *Merchant of Venice*, he shows us how an ordinary night sky is extraordinary to the eye that can behold the gift that every moment holds within itself:

> Look how the floor of heaven
> Is thick inlaid with patines of bright gold:
> There's not the smallest orb which thou behold'st
> But in his motion like an angel sings.[8]

In Shakespeare's imaginative vision, each star was like a paten, a glittering image of God's sacrificial and generous love. He saw with clarity how the intricate and vast harmonies of the universe give witness to the glory of their Creator. This enchanted view of the world is no less real than our scientifically shaped perspectives. Indeed, a certainty of the divine ground of all that exists is the basis of any world that could possibly be understood by science. But we must have ears to hear and eyes to see such wonders.

When we offer sacrifices to God, especially when those sacrifices are offered in union with the sacrifice of the Mass, we are doing something elemental, something as true to our being human as art, music, laughter, mourning, and joy. We join our offerings—all we have—to a new and higher harmony of grace.

The Morning Offering helps us remember that Christ isn't some faraway guide who points out the path and then watches us scramble and trip in more or less the right direction. By entering into his offering of offerings that is the Mass, we let our guide's life become woven into our own. We see the light of his truth even as the morning star rises in our own hearts (2 Pt 1:19).

The Author of our nature has from all eternity willed for us this supernatural destiny: eternal life as children of God by virtue of Christ's offering to the Father. In this sense, the Morning Offering is like a door set close to our heart. Faith is the key that opens for us the countless opportunities to offer God the day we sometimes mistakenly refer to as our own.

Morning Offering in History

Even though it's a short prayer, the Morning Offering has spiritual depth directly stemming from its origins. As we will see, this prayer was born in the heart of a priest who lived the Mass. In this sense, it's a great way to fight discouragement in the spiritual life. How easy it is for us to think, I will always have this defect, or that bad habit, or that temptation. Obstacles or difficulties in marriage, at work, or in the family can seem like boulders, impossible to move on our own. And in many ways, that would be true. On our own we can do nothing (Jn 15:5). But by offering everything—and I mean everything—to God through the sacrifice of the Mass, every day is a new reason to hope because every day sees countless renewals of Christ's gift of himself to the Father on our behalf.

A glance at salvation history will show us offerings punctuating every part of the day. Going back to their earliest history, the Jewish people praised the Lord daily in three distinct moments: the Ma'ariv (evening prayer), Shacharit (morning prayer), and the Minchah (afternoon prayer). Abraham is said to have instituted the first (Gn 22:3), Isaac the second (Gn 24:63), and Jacob the third (Gn 28:11).[9] Each of these moments involve intimate conversation with the Lord, as did recitation of the Shema, Israel's declaration of faith in the one God, the Lord of heaven and earth, and his dominion over all that exists.

As a penitential psalm of David recounts, a contrite heart must be the source of all offered sacrifice: "For thou hast no delight in sacrifice; were I to give a burnt offering, thou wouldst not be pleased. The sacrifice acceptable to God is a broken spirit; a broken and contrite heart, O God, thou wilt not despise" (Ps 51:16–17). Approximately four centuries before Christ, the prophet Malachi warned Israel of the need to offer pure sacrifices from a pure heart: "O priests, who despise my name. You say, 'How have we despised thy name?' By offering polluted food upon my altar" (Mal 1:6–7). The other prophets speak similar rebukes, notably Isaiah 1:11–17 and Amos 5:21–25, in their pleas to unite worship and holiness of life into a single, living unity.

In the Old Testament book of Malachi we see a hint of another, indestructibly pure offering, which will be offered throughout the world: "For from the rising of the sun to its setting my name is great among the nations, and in every place incense is offered to my name, and a pure offering; for my name is great among the nations, says the Lord of hosts" (Mal 1:11).

What sacrifice could this be, notable for its worldwide scope and spotless purity? The fulfillment of the prophecy of Malachi is the holy sacrifice of the Mass.

After centuries of sin offerings, all incomplete, the incarnate Son of God instituted a New Covenant in his blood, anticipating at the Last Supper his sacrifice on the Cross, the central redemptive act of Calvary. On Catholic altars around the world, this great mystery is liturgically enriched and sacramentally renewed, offered to God the Father for the forgiveness of sins.

Neither the doubts expressed in the Protestant Reformation nor the abuse of its gifts by its own members has shaken the Church's dedication to the Eucharist. At various times, when certain truths were neglected, or not loved enough, the Holy Spirit has sent an antidote, a Benedict, a Francis, a Thomas, an Ignatius, a Theresa, a Pius, a John Paul, and many others bearing less famous names, as beacons, reflections of divine light for the Church and the world.

In 1844, in Vals, France, famous for its rejuvenating natural baths, Francois Xavier Gautrelet, S.J., was one such soul. He was a spiritual director at a seminary in Vals at a time when Jesuit missionaries where flooding America and India in the same spirit that St. Francis Xavier stormed Asia three centuries before. Father Francois was appointed director at the relatively young age of thirty-five, a witness to his maturity and spiritual judgment.

Father Francois founded the Apostleship of Prayer on December 3, 1844, for his seminarians with this offering as its cornerstone.[10] In 1852, he was appointed rector of the seminary. His life saw hardships and suffering, borne with fortitude, including being banished from France with his fellow Jesuits due to the many political upheavals of the time. He spent some fruitful years in the Holy Land, becoming the superior of the Jesuit Mission in Syria. All who knew him remember his intense devotion to the Blessed Sacrament. It was said that when he celebrated Holy Mass, his face shone with a glow that was not of this world. Father Francois's life became an offering to God. When he died in 1887, he left this earth with a widespread reputation for sanctity.

Within a few years of the founding of the Apostleship of Prayer, Father Henri Ramiere, one of Gautrelet's students at Vals, became director of the association. Ramiere was an eloquent writer, having studied rhetoric at the Sorbonne.[11] It was Father Henri who intuited that the Morning Offering is intrinsically linked to devotion to the Sacred Heart of Jesus. By 1861, he was living out the Morning Offering in a wide variety of contexts, including parish life and religious communities, as well as editing a magazine dedicated to the

Sacred Heart. Father Henri died in 1884, a tireless worker in helping souls discover the depths of God's mercy.

On October 15, 1885, a twelve-year-old girl in France joined the Apostleship of Prayer and began offering her day with all its joys and sacrifices in union with the pope for the conversion of souls throughout the world. Marie-Françoise-Thérèse Martin continued this practice for the rest of her short life. Now known as St. Thérèse of Lisieux, or the Little Flower, St. Pius X called her "the greatest saint of modern times."[12] Her "little way" of holiness had at its core this daily offering of ordinary life, made holy by giving everything to God. In the 1880s, Pope Leo XIII, inspired by this devotion and its growing popularity, started the tradition of explicitly forming monthly papal intentions. In 1929, Pius XI added a missionary intention. In 1951, Pius XII saw in the Morning Offering an "activation" of the powers implanted in the soul at Baptism.

In 1985, Pope John Paul II called the Apostleship of Prayer "a precious treasure from the Pope's heart and the Heart of Christ."[13] As recently as 2005, a synod of bishops on the Eucharist specifically mentioned the Morning Offering as a way of developing a more profound Eucharistic piety that "is the origin of every form of holiness."[14]

As of 2009, there were over fifty million members in this ministry who practiced the devotion of the Morning Offering. There are also other families within the Church who have a devotion to this prayer, including Opus Dei, founded by St. Josemaría Escrivá and found in countries from Asia to Africa, Europe, and the United States, who seek to offer their entire day as an offering to God. According to James Kubicki, S.J., the national director of the Apostleship of Prayer, in 2014, the general and specific intentions of the Holy Father will be renamed, the first becoming a *universal* intention for the world and the other becoming one for *evangelization* of every soul and every nation.

The Morning Offering, while not formulated as such until the nineteenth century, is implicitly present behind the apostles and early followers of Jesus offering their sufferings to further the growth of the Church. Pharisee Gamaliel's wise counsel—if this message of the apostles were divine in origin nothing could stop it—was seasoned with violence by the Sanhedrin: "And when they had called in the apostles, they beat them and charged them not to speak in the name of Jesus, and let them go. Then they left the presence of the council, rejoicing that they were counted worthy to suffer dishonor for the name" (Acts 5:40–41).

The brutality with which the ancient world dealt with Christians and the consequent holy joy with which these early followers of Christ met their deaths defy natural explanation. In a world that knew the cruelty of the Roman Empire, the stoic's suicide, and the carnality of pagan temples, this "rejoicing" was something altogether new.

But how can an offering to God transform suffering into joy? Such a miracle could only happen after an encounter with the living God.

1. Jesus

"I wasn't there so I can't say He didn't," The Misfit said. "I wisht I had of been there," he said, hitting the ground with his fist. "It ain't right I wasn't there because if I had of been there I would of known. Listen lady," he said in a high voice, "if I had of been there I would of known and I wouldn't be like I am now."

—Flannery O'Connor, *A Good Man Is Hard to Find*

This passage from O'Connor's short story is a good place to start our reflection on the name of Jesus and why the Morning Offering invokes his name in its first breath. There is usually in the life of a believer, at one time or another, a glance toward the voices of doubt as they rise and fall in volume like a conversation on the edge of a great darkness—a glance perhaps, but never a nod. Though the circumstances change over time, ideologies that restrict all reality to human measure tend to follow the same well-worn paths.

Nevertheless, the Misfit in this story, a serial killer who has his men shoot a whole family to obtain a getaway car, does ask some potent questions: Why wasn't the Lord's Resurrection witnessed by all of Jerusalem? Why weren't we there when Lazarus was raised? If we witnessed a miracle, then we wouldn't need this thing called faith. We'd know and be different from what we are now. Even if we aren't killers, that can sound like an awfully good deal.

Would the Misfit really have been different had he seen a miracle of Our Lord's? The question isn't really answerable, of course, but the odds are against it. He is a murderer who seeks to evade responsibility, and when it comes to handing the blame for his life to someone else, Jesus is as convenient a figure as anyone. For many did see, with their own eyes, Lazarus stumble out of his grave at the command of Jesus. Many more saw Lazarus, alive, after his burial. And what was their reaction? The number of disciples grew. Yet the number of Pharisees who wanted to kill Jesus because of this miracle also grew (Jn 11:53).

Here is proof that though the life of faith involves both heart and intellect, how often the heart has the trump card: for it shows what we love. In the Incarnation, truth reveals itself in the person of Jesus. Truth in this way greets us with a face at once recognizable and utterly mysterious. We meet in Jesus not a concept or a theory but a person who is Lord of all that is.

Seeking Christ, therefore, is different from seeking anyone else: the harvest of our efforts depends, in the end, on our willingness to allow truth's splendor to cast its light within us. When we seek primarily ourselves, our light—our guiding star, so to speak—becomes darkness. Even amid advanced technological cultures, one may be blind to the way that leads to Christ. Thus the "lamp" of the person's choosing becomes "light" only when the innermost core of that person lies open to what is, even at the risk of suffering (Mt 6:23). This is why God's "weakness" is stronger than humanity: it shows, with divine rigor, what each of us is in our innermost being.

Blessed John Henry Newman makes this aspect of believing especially clear in his sermon "Faith and Reason, Contrasted as Habits of Mind," preached when he was an Anglican, on the Feast of the Epiphany, in 1839. In this eloquent meditation on the "home" of Faith, which is the "heart itself," Newman explores the various ways that Faith is either embraced or rejected by the individual when a miracle is presented to the senses. To those who think belief or unbelief simply a natural matter, unconnected to our moral being, Newman forcefully objects: "But a man *is* responsible for his faith, because he is responsible for his likings and dislikings, his hopes and his opinions, on all of which his faith depends."[1]

This brings us to a paradox: Faith in Jesus Christ is at once mediated and the most intimate of relationships. Though Christ touches each soul directly in the life of Faith and especially in the Eucharist, Dom Jean-Baptiste Chautard reminds us about "the universal law laid down by Providence" that it is through others—principally, the Church, of course—that we find the way to salvation.[2] This should not surprise us. If we would know any history, we must establish reliable records from the past. If we would benefit from the medicines invented by geniuses, we have to have a reasonable trust in their expertise. How much more, then, does the search for the Lord demand more than our own personal resources, no matter how richly gifted they might be?

The Misfit in O'Connor's story, as we have seen, completely misunderstands the nature of faith. He thinks seeing would conquer all doubts. But this is not true. Just as the Pharisees were incensed over the miracle of Lazarus's rising from the tomb, so we are told that some of the apostles were, at least initially, "doubtful" when the risen Lord appeared to them on the mountain (Mt 28:17). There is no getting around the heart and its openness or hostility to faith.

By his very nature, the Lord God outstrips our capacity for grasping shreds of certainty too small for his infinite being. But because of the Incarnation, this same God has drawn close and can be known by Faith, itself a journey that will only end in the unendingness of eternal life. Roch Kereszty rightly singles out the Apostle John for being the first to see the risen Christ when the apostles were on the sea of Tiberias: "His faith makes him sharp-sighted."[3] Moreover, as Aquinas points out, there is no certainty greater than Faith because Faith is based on the authority of Almighty God, who cannot deceive or be deceived.[4]

Kereszty notes this perennial characteristic of Christ: "He has become the sign of contradiction from his birth to our own day. No one who studies his life and teaching can maintain a credibly indifferent posture."[5] The richness of his being—both God and man, bringer of peace and division, the Word made flesh, and eternal reason speaking with a Galilean accent—demands a response that is total. Scholarly diffidence, skeptical urbanity, and humanistic appreciation all miss the nature of his claim, and hence also miss him entirely.

Part of the reality of faith in Christ originates in the nature of the human person. We are beings who can know, who can trust, and who can be faithful to a divine promise. Polish poet Czeslaw Milosz has observed that there are two dramatically different ways to see the human person: either as a thinking offshoot of a piece of cosmic mold or as a cathedral.[6]

Those who hold to the former ironically don't realize that mold, no matter how advanced, cannot entertain cosmological theories. The cathedral image, of course, is deeply consonant with the riches of interiority open to even the humblest person. It is reminiscent of the Christian idea of the individual believer as "a temple of the Holy Spirit" (1 Cor 6:19). This interior life may be rich and luminous, or darkened with sin and self-love, "bare ruined choirs," hungering for a new sensation or experience to ease the pain of often self-inflicted inner poverty.

The first breath of our Morning Offering rightly belongs to Our Lord, and it does so primarily in regard to his priesthood. He is not merely an exalted model for future human endeavors, or just a rich personality such as Socrates who engages our thought with his own particular human brilliance. He is the eternal Word, incarnate of the Virgin Mary, Jesus of Nazareth, the Christ.

In an essay published in *Communio* in 1990, Benedict XVI gives us something of a preview of his later, three-volume *Jesus of Nazareth*. In both works, Benedict outlines a broad but profound understanding of Christ as the culmination of God's exodus, of the leading out of fallen humanity from sin and death. In taking hold of this liberation, one must be able to allow Christ to unfold, as it were, in his human and divine reality: one must have the openness to the past, with an ability to hear its promises as they are voiced anew today. As well, one must recognize the incursion of the eternal into our lives with its ability to speak a word that remains valid for all time. As Benedict reminds us, echoing St. Paul, Christ is "the same yesterday and today and forever" (Heb 13:8).

In this way, Christ is not diminished according to our preconceived ideas. Benedict dismisses any "following" of Christ's way that does not include the way of the Cross: "No, the call to following concerns not just some human program, or the human virtues of Jesus, but his *entire* way, 'through the curtain' (Heb 10:20). What is essential and new about the way of Jesus Christ is that he opens *this* way for us, for only thus do we come into freedom. The meaning of 'following' is to enter into communion with God."[7]

That curtain is "his flesh." The way of discipleship involves at its core a following of Jesus' flesh on the Cross, a dying to self, and a consequent rising up in the grace of the paschal mystery. This includes the sacramental life, with its simplicity, humility, and depthless intimacy that will only blossom in eternity when the pilgrim Church becomes transfigured into "a new heaven and a new earth" (Rv 21:1), and "death shall be no more" (Rv 21:4).

When our first parents failed to grasp the gift of each moment streaming from God's goodness, in pride they chose the lie that their dependence on that goodness was somehow demeaning to their dignity. The images of the visible world ever since then have lulled us into believing that a finite good—something created—can satisfy our yearning for truth, for happiness, and for God.

Whom do we see when we look at Jesus Christ? He who sees Christ, writes Benedict, sees "the Father, and the entire trinitarian mystery. For we must add, when one sees the Father in Christ, then in him the veil of the temple is truly rent, and the interior of God is laid bare. For then the one and only God is visible not as a monad, but as Trinity. Then man truly becomes a friend, initiated into the innermost mystery of God."[8]

When we look to Christ, we see something both conceivable (for it happened) and inconceivable by human reason alone. Yet in this, we also see the mystery of our personhood illuminated in a light without ending. Here, in a passage that St. John Paul II loved to reference, is the unfailing source of human dignity and freedom: "The truth is that only in the mystery of the incarnate Word does the mystery of man take on light. For Adam, the first man, was a figure of Him Who was to come, namely Christ the Lord. Christ, the final Adam, by the revelation of the mystery of the Father and His love, fully reveals man to man himself and makes his supreme calling clear. It is not surprising, then, that in Him all the aforementioned truths find their root and attain their crown."[9] Notice how John Paul finds this crown not on humanity but on Christ, the Alpha and Omega, God's eternal Word made man, the new Adam. What started on a quiet Sunday morning—though foreseen from eternity—offers us now a new life of grace, rooted and perfected in God's very life.

Bending our knee before the Lord of heaven and earth, we see here one greater than any prophet, one whom Solomon, at the height of his wisdom, would have given kingdoms to see. But we see him with the eyes of faith. Better yet, "we have the mind of Christ" (1 Cor 2:16) when we live by his Spirit.

A Morning Prayer

So having seen the hurdles of errant reason as little more than mirages, designed to confuse, I find you, Lord. In a world where knowledge has become data, steaming in the invisible jungles of chatter in which we move, forget, and have our being, you await us, patient for more than twenty centuries. In my insufficiency, the very nature of which I at times so dread, I find you.

You answer my yearning for the reason of my existence better than a spring of cool water can quench agonizing thirst. My soul (a tangled, tattered garment, once wedding white, now sometimes unrecognizable by my own chosen self-damage) is given by your grace the thrilling flutter of repose; it is a maple tree on an October day, alive to its own beautiful dying and relishing the transformation that will bring me to a sky of unending adoration before your face.

You bestow the gift of yourself on all who seek you and are fired from within by your holiness; this holiness which touched the ineffably bright eternity of its goodness and let time and space rollick outward into days unending, days that are the seedbed of souls you take to yourself. O Jesus, what true joy does not sing your name?

You walk with me through my poor man's dying into your warm embrace, waiting from all eternity. This is not the blank eternity of impersonality but the "heart's embrace" of the Father's eternal love of his Son, endlessly taken up by the Holy Spirit in the contemplation of the love that gives without loss, that loves without passion, that fills without satiation, and that blooms galaxies and tulips simply because you are good without end, beautiful beyond my heart's deepest longing.

Your love fills my heart with sentiments of love and devotion, and inspires my will to acts of self-sacrifice that find no natural explanation, heartened by centuries of self-abnegation and lifetimes of quiet self-sacrifice, alongside the

glorious, torch-like charity of countless martyrs. You fill me
with not only sentiments but also virtues, infused strengths
that adorn the soul like gems lit with heaven's fire.

You meet us in the solemn proclamation of your gospels, handed down by our mother the Church like a string of
pearls, formed in the dark hours of martyrdom and luminous
with an unearthly light. We meet you in the breathing icon of
your very self, each soul conceived in your image.

You meet us, above all, in the liturgical renewal of your
total victory on Mount Calvary, Holy Mass. Here, in the *fons et
culmen*, the source and summit of the Christian's life according to the Second Vatican Council, we find you in the sweetness, wisdom, and chaste beauty of your bride, the Church.
Whether offered at High Mass at Chartres Cathedral or in a
prison cell, you would have us join you on Calvary, all our
sufferings now yours, all our offerings now yours, and your
triumph now ours—in hope, so we may, in eternity, become
"sharers" in your "divinity."[10]

You have not left us, either: "Lo, I am with you always"
(Mt 28:20). With Blessed Newman, we watch the tabernacle
light with undimmed hope: "Nothing moves there but the
distant glimmering Lamp which betokens the Presence of our
Undying Life, hidden yet ever working."[11]

Approaching the Mystery

Here is the *mysterium fidei* by which we live. Nothing, perhaps,
gives more of what Newman called a sense of objective reality
to Catholicism than this faith in the Real Presence of Christ in
the Eucharist. It is chiefly this manner of his presence, masked
by the appearances of the food of the poor, which can break
open the heart of the proud when they kneel before him, the
Lord of all. Others may entertain theories about the deity;
we will come and adore him. Jesus has become small so we
may draw close and speak with him words addressed to no

other as we partake of that conversation of the Father, Son, and Holy Spirit that is the heart of prayer.

This God now has a name always new. Above all other names, it is the only name under heaven that can save us (Acts 4:12). We speak it with reverence and with the same breath that we offer to him this day.

2. Immaculate Heart

For we know who God is in the faces of those who belong to him.

—Pope Benedict XVI

No one belongs to the Lord as does his Mother. Here, in the very first words of the Morning Offering, we express a joyful reality that at once speaks of God's omnipotence and the intimacy of his definitive entrance into history. Every soul that comes into the world, from the worldly man of power to the nameless one lost in poverty, is born of a mother. We are held below our mother's heart for nine months, a dependency that the modern world has decided to leave hanging by the thread of the mother's will. Yet God, from all eternity, has spoken another word by means of this very dependency—a definitive "yes" to his promises made to humanity since the world began (2 Cor 1:20), a word that was not uttered in vain (Is 55:11).

Two thousand years ago, before the reverent awe of an angelic presence, the Word of God became incarnate in the womb of Mary, a virgin from Nazareth. He who holds all times and places in his hand, who "dwells in unapproachable light" (1 Tm 6:16), chose for his Son a mother. This quiet moment in a dusty outpost of the Roman Empire should bring great joy to our souls. Its mystery glows with a splendor of undying brilliance.

Our Lady is an invaluable help in our efforts to offer everything to God. She is a woman of promise from the very beginning of the human story, for she is the bearer of that offspring that will crush the head of the sterile tempter (Gn 3:15). Mary is a model of the Church in the manner of her perfect union with Christ and in her maternal heart, so rich with faith, hope, and love.[1] By her simplicity before the Angel Gabriel, even as she saw herself blessed with many gifts, she opened her heart and, in this way, the door of the world to the Incarnation, the Redemption, the apostles, the Church, the sacraments, and the saints of every age who have lived the will of her Son in filial imitation of her Immaculate Heart.

The Virgin Mary is the loving witness to God's refusal to give up on a world beautiful in its core but wayward in its stubborn folly.

As has been frequently noted, Our Lady's Immaculate Heart is prefigured in various images and persons in the Old Testament. She is foreseen in the ark of the Lord (Ex 40:34–35), which held within it the Ten Commandments carved on stone tablets, the heavenly manna, and Aaron's rod—the latter an image of death and resurrection in its resprouting (Heb 9:5).[2] The ark had a cloud that "overshadowed" it, while Mary has the Archangel Gabriel's promise that the "Holy Spirit will come upon you, and the power of the Most High will overshadow you" (Lk 1:35). The ark of the Lord was made of precious wood and gold, with a golden crown (Ex 25:11), while Our Lady was free from the stain of original sin from the first moment of her conception, her soul rich with infused virtues. Just as the law went from being struck on stone tablets to being engraved on our hearts through grace, so the ark foreshadows Our Lady as the dwelling place of the Lord's presence in her virginal womb.

Our Lady is the crowning "yes" to the countless number of God's promises fulfilled in her son, Jesus Christ. She is Virgin and Mother (Is 7:14). Through her giving birth in Bethlehem, the universal promise of Israel will flourish "to the ends of the earth" by virtue of her divine Son, who will "stand and feed his flock in the strength of the Lord" (Mi 5:2–4). God's promise in Genesis 3:15 becomes reality in the physical and spiritual maternity of the Mother of God. So great is this commission of hers from God that it tolls like a great, solemn bell from one end of the scripture and Tradition to the other.

This is why Our Lady's heart is the perfect accompaniment to our Morning Offering. God has willed this from all eternity, from the misstep of our first parents right up to his last moments on the Cross: "Behold, your mother" (Jn 19:27). We cannot separate what God has joined. When we seek to offer our day to God, we will always find our Mother waiting for us.

One of the ways Mary teaches us to offer everything to God is by her example of always turning toward the Lord. Her nobility is a finely balanced character (a balance only attained by grace) that knows incredible joy, shattering sorrow, and a faith in God that doesn't bend, no matter what. Her joy at the presentation of her child in the Temple is tempered by Simeon's prophecy: "And a sword will pierce through your own soul also, that thoughts out of many hearts may be revealed" (Lk 2:35). As Archbishop Fulton Sheen pointed out, "From the moment she heard Simeon's words, she would never again lift the Child's hands without seeing a shadow of nails on them; every sunset would be a blood-red image of His Passion."[3]

When we bring our sufferings and burdens to Our Lady so she may assist us in offering them to the Lord, we need never fear that somehow she won't be able to sympathize with our plight. The sorrows of her life touched her innocent heart with ineffable pain, and as she sanctified her heart the more by offering it in union with her Son's sufferings on the Cross, she will teach us to do the same.

These are just a few of the reasons the Morning Offering puts the Immaculate Heart so close to its first breath. Mary is, after Our Lord's sacred humanity, the most ennobled soul in the history of the world. She is so thoroughly a mother to her children adopted by grace that no suffering, no hardship, and not even the worst sin can repel her maternal care.

In all of this, her Immaculate Heart is completely free from sentimentality, from selfish indulgence, and from self-deluded thinking that somehow God's moral laws are in any way inconsistent with his charity. Indeed, as with the burning bush that proclaimed the Decalogue to Moses, brilliant with light but unconsumed because of partaking purely of the undying truth, Mary brings the realism of love to her Morning Offering.

This love of hers, a gift of God, is the love that moves the sun and the stars; this love believes all, even in the cold, meager light of a manger; even in exile in Egypt, fleeing the gaze of a murderous king; during the bloody climb to Calvary; at the final, agonized offering of her Son's sacrifice on the Cross that flung open the doors of heaven; or during the hope-filled vigil of Holy Saturday—all these hours schooled Mary's heart in how to make each day a perfect offering to Our Lord.

Our Lady is the mystical spouse of the Holy Spirit, and the new Eve for a redeemed humanity. Her fidelity to the Word of God is her primary claim to the humility that is also her greatness. This can best be expressed only in silence and in song. For this very reason, her maternal care for us is particularly realized when we see her as the model of liturgical worship. In the homilies of St. Bernard of Clairvaux (1190–1153), we see the Virgin taking precisely this role. Our Lady speaks for the Church, of which she is the Mother, and the praise that flows from her every word and action expresses a heavenly eloquence beautiful beyond words.

St. Bernard, in his *Homilies in Praise of the Blessed Virgin Mary*, writes, "The New Song which only virgins will have the right to sing in the kingdom of God will certainly be sung by the Queen of Virgins and she will certainly be the first one to intone it."[4] While it is true that this *canticum novum* is sung in Revelation 14:3 by men who have not married, Bernard's point is sound in the sense that the heavenly court, with liturgical and spiritual symbols abounding, is preeminently a place of unending praise.

Our Lady plays a key role in this rich image of the consummation of time as it is brought into the eternity of God. Indeed, all of the Christological mysteries come by way of the Virgin's Immaculate Heart, and so it is fitting that she would lead us in this new song where all our tears are wiped away by the divine tenderness.

Our Lady is a model of liturgical worship because her "soul magnifies the Lord" (Lk 1:46). She embodies adoration, thanksgiving, and petition in every beating of her heart, and she pleads for reparation—not for her sake, as she is without sin—but for us, her children. Her Immaculate Heart was deepened in its experience of those who are without God, and what petty cruelties and major horrors we can commit. Our Lady is therefore a compass setting, as it were, for proper worship of God.

All superficiality, all glib optimism, and all egotism fly from her presence. She gives witness to the *rationabile obsequium*, that "spiritual worship" that should be at the core of all liturgical prayer (Rom 12:1). Our Lady is not the giver of song that humanity sings in this vale of tears but a witness to that consoling foretaste of the praise which rises up to God. Benedict XVI has written of this "sober inebriation" that exceeds "all the possibilities of mere reason," rightly pointing out that it is a gift of the Spirit.[5] Who else could better intone such song—its beauty the glow of the true and the good when embraced—than Our Lady, spouse of the Holy Spirit?

Here we again find Our Lady's heart giving us a living icon of that offering of love of which God never tires. Our prayer, our suffering, our joys, and our sorrows should pass through the Immaculate Heart of Mary. She will teach us to sing with the mystical Body of Christ, the Church, in a humble, rich harmony singularly free of self-seeking, a perfect integration of the Word into our own hearts and lives.

The Morning Offering, always looking toward the Cross, is the sure path to this reality, avoiding as it does the pitfalls of activism and the prideful preening of moralism. The very *act of offering* is like a lance into the heart of our pride (which will be defeated only on the other side of the grave), making us cry out with St. Paul, "I have been crucified with Christ; and it is no longer I who live, but Christ who lives in me" (Gal 2:20). As Our Lady's very being "magnified the Lord," so her intercession will infuse into our sometimes painful offerings a note of joy. As St. Josemaría Escrivá put it, "Before, by yourself, you couldn't. Now, you've turned to Our Lady, with her, how easy!"[6] It is easy only because she helps us and because her maternal care brings us her risen Son, food for our hungry souls.

Think of the French writer Paul Claudel's experience while listening to the singing of the Magnificat during Vespers at Christmas in the Cathedral of Notre Dame in Paris in 1886: "In that moment," he wrote, "an event happened that dominates my whole life. In an instant my heart was touched and I believed. I believed with a force of adhesion so great, with such a lifting of all my being, with a conviction so powerful, in a certainty that would not leave room for any kind of doubt that, from that point onward, no reasoning, no circumstance of my agitated life could either shake my faith or touch it."[7]

What confidence can be born in a single moment! Such confidence can arise to bring light and grace to an entire life but only when we live day by day, minute by minute, giving up everything for the pearl of eternity. Our Lady has made many a simple moment rich with the frankincense and myrrh of her heart's desire, that purest of offerings, so close to the heart of her Son. Only in eternity will the whole song of her favors be sung.

In the Morning Offering, we will utter her name with filial love and trust, knowing that she will not fail us. Our mother will teach us to sing, to turn our sorrows to joy, by offering everything with her to Our Lord. This morning can then be prelude to that praise that will never end.

3. Prayers

For we pray not that we may change Divine decree, but only to obtain what God has decided will be obtained through prayer. In other words, as St. Gregory says, "that by asking, men may deserve to receive what Almighty God has decreed from all eternity to give them."

—St. Thomas Aquinas [1]

In our Morning Offering we offer all the prayers we make this day to the Lord. The act of offering everything to God seals, as it were, our gift with at least the will to praise our Creator, and not ourselves.

How often I have seen myself doing what is surely a common occurrence for many Catholics: after months, maybe even years, of praying for something or for someone, in the end I realize I have in fact been trying to bend God's will to my own. How foolish! Part of every genuine prayer lies in the *acceptance* of everything that comes from God's providence, no matter how painful or mysterious. Otherwise, we risk the entire point of prayer, which is being taken into the endless intimacy of the Holy Trinity both now during our wayfaring in this beautiful, fractured world and for eternity when the yearning of every sincere prayer will see its everlasting reward.

19

But until then, the Morning Offering is a way to protect ourselves from the self-satisfactions of a prideful heart, pleased at its own virtues. Because all the hours and minutes of our day, even the sweetness or the dryness of prayer, are ultimately a gift of God meant to purify us, it is only right we give to the Lord an offering of praise, which acknowledges his goodness as the source of everything and his providence as tending to the least sparrow that falls to the ground. In times of joy, this offering protects us from self-sufficiency and pride, and in times of sorrow, it will rescue us from despair.

In describing briefly the offering of our prayers to the Lord, we should all echo the Master's words, "My teaching is not mine, but his who sent me" (Jn 7:16). While the Church's saints are also teachers of the life of prayer, this is so primarily because of their intimacy with the Teacher of prayer, Jesus Christ. As the Father has sent his Son, who brings into our world the unbreakable promises of God, so the prayerful soul is one that is allied to the Heart of the World. Christ is the one and only Teacher of prayer. It is from him that we all must learn.

Jesus as the second person of the Holy Trinity become incarnate has from the moment of his conception enjoyed the beatific vision. This drawing up of humanity in the intimacy of God was foreseen from all eternity. Jesus' person is a divine person, with no confusions or barriers to this singular relationship he now enjoys in heaven. His self-emptying did not mean he left off being God; his sufferings were an act of one person, perfectly human and perfectly divine. The Word-become-flesh is our Emmanuel, and therefore, as God-with-us, he is the life of all prayer, of all communion with God.

Of course, the first disciples did not start from this lofty height when they first encountered Jesus. He took care to bring them into friendship with himself and gradually reveal, to those who could receive it, the real nature of who he is. Indeed, Jesus often waits for the disciples to ask in order to respect their freedom as well as to work with them in both a human and a divine manner. Luke shows us this in a marvelously simple way when "one of his disciples," after seeing Jesus pray, asks, "Lord, teach us to pray, as John taught his disciples" (Lk 11:1). As everyone knows, Jesus responds with the Our Father.

According to St. Augustine, this one prayer contains within it the *whole* breadth of prayer itself, for "we say nothing that is not found in this prayer of the Lord, if we pray properly and fittingly."[2]

But what does it mean to pray properly?

Augustine reminds us, in a letter to a prominent Roman widow, in the year AD 412 or so, that the Lord knows what we need before we ask, as Jesus tells us in Luke's gospel. But by praying to God, we become able to receive what he desires to give us through prayer. In general, it is good to be relieved of suffering—personal faults, illness afflicting ourselves or our loved ones, financial difficulties, deep-seated challenges in our marriages, doubts, perhaps about our vocation, and so forth—and so we pray for deliverance from these things. We should wish, of course, not for a superficial deliverance so we won't be troubled but to better realize God's will on earth.

Yet sometimes, even after years of faithful prayer, we get no answer. Augustine would here point out that, after all, such trials in life may well be exactly what we need to secure our salvation. As nothing in this life can compare to *that*, we can find hope in knowing that all things work for the good of those who love God (Rom 8:28). This, of course, is easier to say than to live.

How often we become frustrated with God for what seems like his indifference to our prayers! Nothing, however, could be further from the truth of who God is. In times of trouble, when prayer seems almost impossible, when it seems as if the universe has just kicked us in the stomach, we must remember that our Father in heaven is infinitely powerful and infinitely good. Perhaps we should simply pray over that word, *infinite*. Only God himself is so. No prayer is therefore unheard, though each answer will be given with infinite wisdom, love itself. God always saves the good wine until last.

Praying "properly" perhaps sounds a little fastidious today. Can we really do something so intimate and personal incorrectly? Who is to say if our prayers are not "done" correctly? For the Christian, it is never a matter of "technique" that renders prayer inadequate, unable to flourish as prayer should.

Throughout our life, as Blessed Dom Columba Marmion puts it, we must look to Jesus in order to learn how to pray: "Christ is God put within our reach, under a human manifestation: it is Divine perfection revealing itself to us under earthly forms; it is holiness itself, appearing in perceptible form to our eyes for thirty-three years, to make itself tangible and imitable. We can never think too much about this. Christ is God making himself man, living among men, so as to make them learn, by his words and above all by his life, how men should imitate God and be pleasing to Him."[3]

This is exactly what the apostles did. They heard the exciting news of Jesus beginning his public ministry, soon after John's dramatic announcement of "he who is to come" (Mt 11:3). They saw the miracles of Jesus with their own eyes; they listened to him preach repentance and the good news that the reign of God was breaking into human history in a way never seen before. They listened to his parables and the explanations that he gave to them, the chosen Twelve. They began to notice his daily habits, his nights of prayer, alone in the hills before the stars of heaven and his Father.

Mark makes special note of his early rising: "In the morning, a great while before day, he rose and went out to a lonely place, and there he prayed" (Mk 1:35). How joyful must have been their realization that, though in a lonely place, Jesus was never alone but always in prayerful communion with his Father, the one who sent him into our world. This is how the apostles learned to pray and how we must learn to pray too, by watching Christ, by loving imitation of his deeds and words, at all times of our life.

Jesus gave his disciples specific guidance in regard to prayer. This guidance, of course, has a timeless relevance for all who wish to talk to God and to listen to his replies: "The prayer of a Christian is never a monologue."[4]

Jesus reminds us never to grow weary in our petitions (Lk 11:5); to never discount the love of the infinite God; to take some time away from our work and preoccupations, as Jesus himself did, for regular prayer (Mk 6:30); to pray in times of gratitude (Lk 10:21), persecution, peril (Lk 12:12); and always, to pray with sincerity and not for human admiration or respect (Mt 6:8).

From these and many other instances in the gospels, we see the formation of the traditional ends of prayer—adoration, petition, intercession, and thanksgiving—all coming together in the person of Christ. Every action of Jesus, every gesture, and every heartbeat is prayer of the most perfect kind. As we grow to resemble him, so will our prayer become more like his, and as our prayer becomes more authentic, so will the life of our soul flow spontaneously from his heart, treasury of all graces and virtues.

In the same way that Christian prayer is not about technique, those souls most experienced in prayer do not forgo simple vocal prayers because they have somehow gone "beyond" them. Vocal prayers such as the Our Father, the Rosary, or the psalms come from the heart of God, not man, and as such contain within themselves mysteries whose riches cannot be fathomed completely in this life. The other traditional forms of prayer—mental prayer and contemplative prayer, including *lectio divina*, the devout pondering of sacred scripture in the presence of God—have their place in the life of a Christian. For many reasons, we should strive to find a wise person, priest or lay, who can guide us in the maturation of this intimacy with God that we call prayer.

For if we want to be saints—and there is no other final goal of our existence—then we must cherish prayer as more important than anything we do. The life of Christ in our souls comes by prayer, graced by the sacraments of the Church and offered to Our Lord on the paten of every moment of every day. If we want to be saints, friends of God, then we must get to know him in prayer.

There is no other way.

We must not be afraid of the silence of prayer and the sense of our own limitedness that comes with it. As we let the noise of the bustle of life quiet down, we can begin to see how much God loves this world of ours, which was created good and broken by sin but redeemed by his precious blood. Taking time out of our day to look at, to welcome inwardly in our hearts, some scene from the gospels or the lives of the saints can bring to us intimations of grace that can redirect or revive our resolutions to seek God in the midst of the world, spreading his peace with all that we do and say.

Prayer is rightly considered a journey because it is never "completed" until we reach our home in heaven. St. Paul, in fact, encourages us to "pray constantly" (1 Thes 5:17). This must be properly understood. A permanent state of vocal prayer, mental prayer, or even direct consideration of divine things will drive us off the rails, not make us saints. Instead, much like the formal intention we make in our Morning Offering, we can make an act of will from the deepest part of our being that will bring to us a prayerful sense of recollection that is the very soul of prayer. As Benedict Baur put it in his 1955 classic work on companionship with God, "Prayer as a condition of soul is . . . a permanent inner attitude of loving surrender to God, a childlike submission to His divine will and providence in all the affairs of our life. It is a constant attitude of compliance, in which our will completely yields itself to God's wishes for us, to whatever He sends us in the way of tasks, duty, rules, or commandments."[5]

So, yes, it is good to use our imaginations to summon a scene from scripture, to try to see that scene in all its human and divine richness. At other times, vocal prayers, said alone or with others, can fill the heart with devotion. Short aspirations—"arrows of prayer" Augustine called them—can act like tinder, setting our hearts ablaze with fervor. Mental prayer—just looking with love on God and his goodness—can lift the mind to the highest truths of our faith, filling our souls with love and awe. But in the crucible of the daily tasks before us, according to our state in life, our vocation, our careers, we must launch into the deep with an attitude of prayer, embracing every element of our day as allowed or willed by Our Lord.

All of God's gifts come through prayer, itself a gift.

At the holy sacrifice of the Mass, the prayer of Christ, and therefore the most perfect prayer, we join our individual prayers to the altar, where "Christ our Redeemer and High Priest continues the work of our redemption in, with, and through His Church" (*CCC*, 1069). Here also we invoke the Holy Spirit, inspirer and perfecter of all prayer and sanctity. While all the "exterior" works of God are done in the unity of the Father, Son, and Holy Spirit, God also desires that we honor the distinction of persons within his inner life.

Hence we are taught by Our Lord himself to befriend the "spirit of truth," the "Consoler," and the "Advocate" who has been given to the Church and to each of us in the sacramental life we enjoy as God's adopted children. This invoking of the Holy Spirit, beseeching him for his sevenfold gifts, ought to be a regular part of our prayer. In times of sorrow, in times of profound loss, and in times of rejoicing and thanksgiving, the Holy Spirit will keep us grounded in the reality of God's inner life.

Though our prayer often bears the dusty traces of our paths through life, we would always do well to remember its lofty nature—to speak with the Creator is a privilege beyond our rights. Many of the ancient pagans saw the world beyond this life as immovable in its eternal fixity and distance. Yet we, by Our Lord's self-emptying, have been offered intimacy with that same eternal God who has left off none of his immensity in drawing close to us, sharing our humanity without trace of sin, in this second springtime for humanity.

"Let me hear in the morning of thy steadfast love, for in thee I put my trust" (Ps 143:8).

4. Works

Make no mistake about it. Man's duty to work is not a consequence of original sin, nor is it just a discovery of modern times. It is an indispensable means which God has entrusted to us here on this earth. It is meant to fill out our days and make us sharers in God's creative power.

—St. Josemaría Escrivá, *Working for God*

In Kazuo Ishiguro's novel *The Remains of the Day*, the narrator Mr. Stevens works for a Lord Darlington as head butler in a fine old English house. The year is 1956. The estate has been sold to an American businessman, and the large staff has been trimmed to a handful of part-time help. With permission of his new employer, Stevens embarks on a short trip to see the former housemaid of Darlington Hall, whom he might have married, except that he gave everything, his whole life, to Lord Darlington. Now in late middle age, Stevens reflects on the choices he has made over the years that have left him, as the novel gradually makes clear, utterly bereft of self-respect, friendship, and the dignity he once believed was at the core of a good butler's work among the grandest names of England's aristocracy.

What separates this novel from many others about the struggles of middle age is Stevens's attitude toward work. He learned from his father, himself a butler, that he must never "abandon" his "professional being" for any reason whatsoever. Only when he is alone, says Stevens, and only "when he wills to do so," may a butler discard his professional zeal, that "dignity in keeping with his station," which is what he believes makes a butler great. This theme is subtly woven into Stevens's narration and makes his story quietly but deeply disturbing.

Ishiguro shows us a man who has in fact made his work into an idol. This results in his blind allegiance to Lord Darlington, whom we later learn was a pawn for the Nazis before the Second World War. Darlington dies a shattered man, his reputation forever ruined by his sympathies with the crackpot ideologies of one of the century's greatest evils.

Stevens gradually discovers that his entire life has been wasted by his dedication to a false ideal. Memories haunt him. We see him remembering his father dying in one of the servant's rooms upstairs while he serves port to the gentleman Lord Darlington has called to the estate to discuss how they can tilt the British government toward more pro-German policies during early 1920s. Unable to cope with the impropriety of his father dying on such an important night for Lord Darlington, Stevens denies the gravity of the moment and leaves his father to die alone. While not an evil man, Stevens has delivered himself over to a code or ethic of work that is entirely self-generated and ultimately dehumanizing.

There is a not a single reference to God in the entire novel. Stevens selflessly works for Lord Darlington, but his single-minded pursuit of work for its own sake, shorn of any transcendent purpose, locks him into a religious pursuit of a merely temporal aim. The result is darkness. Each "triumph" Stevens celebrates is ironically a catastrophe for his humanity.

Zeal, sweat, effort, dedication, and perseverance must all be illuminated by the true purpose of work if that labor is to be fruitful in a supernatural sense. Sacrifice is wasted when it is for a false ideal or for self. We must not be like Stevens, perfect in everything but the aim and motive of all our efforts.

To understand work, Christians start with Genesis 1:28, when God spoke his first word to humanity, to our first parents: "And God blessed them, and God said to them, 'Be fruitful and multiply, and fill the earth and subdue it; and have dominion over the fish of the sea and over the birds of the air and over every living thing that moves upon the earth." This is the charter, so to speak, for all serious reflection on the nature of human work in relation to man's final end. Humanity must realize that, among the visible creation, we alone bring intellect and will to all we touch.

The life of animals and all inanimate creation gives glory to God by material laws, or the promptings of instinct, which in their own way show forth the Creator's wisdom but on a completely different plane from the person. We are called to a higher level of existence, one that is infused with the mystery of freedom. And freedom must embrace the truth to flourish.

Because of the fall of our first parents, of course, we earn our bread "in the sweat of our brow." Due to a misuse of human freedom at the dawn of our race, difficulties within—from sloth and from our distaste for effort—and without—the often intractable nature of the objects of our labor—have characterized all work. This reality, however, has not stopped countless cultures from producing magnificent cultural achievements, often, sadly, from slave labor, showing both the glory and the weakness of humanity itself.

With the Incarnation of Christ—the Word-made-flesh, the second person of the Blessed Trinity, born of a virgin—all humanity became ennobled, at least potentially, by this unprecedented condescension of our Creator. Born in poverty in a shepherd's cave, in an obscure outpost of the Roman Empire, Our Lord quietly but radically changed our world on that first Christmas morning. As G. K. Chesterton put it in *The Everlasting Man*, when God was born in the outlying precincts of Bethlehem, "after that moment there could be no slaves."[1]

Though it would take centuries before the noxious weed of slavery was uprooted, the ultimate motive for the dignity of all humanity took place there, amid the steaming breaths of cattle and the cold comfort of straw.

This Gospel was good news indeed, and it overturned the old prejudices of a world that could not imagine the humility of God taking flesh. It was a revolution from within, and it grew like the mustard seed in the hearts of all who heard the good news and responded to this teaching that death was not the end, that suffering could redeem, and that this man who was God has died and come back and now everything is different, though outwardly nothing has changed.

Yet in the world of politics much had changed as countless northern European tribes migrated across Europe, bringing with them fire and chaos. With the collapse of the Roman Empire in AD 476, there rose up in the West monasteries founded in the early fifth century by St. Benedict. With the institution of his Rule, a model of brevity and practical wisdom, men fled the corruptions of the crumbling empire in search of God in the seclusion of the monastery. *Ora et labora* became their motto as they prayed and worked for God. Their life became a model of communal living, an inspiration of democratic governance, and a radical retreat from the godless forces running amok in the remnants of a fallen empire.

One cannot underestimate the beneficial effect such monasteries have had in the last 1,500 years. At the height of the Benedictine influence, there were more than thirty-six thousand monasteries throughout Europe.[2] During the medieval years of reform, under the Cistercians, swamps were turned into world-class vineyards, the Church found a steady source of prelates and priests, and the quiet prayer of the monks interceded for souls everywhere.

Nevertheless, this flight from the world, along with the old feudal divisions of society that tended to focus on religious vocations as the main path to sanctity, meant that a theology of work for the laity would have to wait until the early twentieth century for full development.

As the Blessed Virgin treasured the life of her divine Son, and pondered it in her heart (Lk 2:19), so has the Church in prayer and reflection drawn fresh insights from the deposit of faith. At its deepest root, this development over the centuries is not, however, merely a human achievement. As Jose Luis Illanes writes, "Great changes and movements in the Church are not the result of natural forces or even of human meditation on the word of God: it is the Holy Spirit who weaves a pattern towards the measure of the fullness of Christ at which the Church aims."[3] One such development, in the early years of the twentieth century, brought forth from a divine source a truth "as old as the Gospel, and like the Gospel, new,"[4] this being nothing else than a rediscovery of the universal call to holiness in the ordinary life of everyday people.

Holy discretion has largely hidden the wonders that were shown to St. Josemaría Escrivá on October 2, 1928, while on retreat in Madrid with the Vincentians. In the quiet of his room, while going over some personal notes, God showed him his plan for what would later be called Opus Dei, the Work of God. This new calling within the Church would have as its core teachings the universal call to holiness and the sanctification of oneself and others in and through one's daily work. Years later, St. Josemaría would say, "The Work burst into the world on that 2nd of October of 1928."[5]

This illumination left Josemaría with a profound sense of God's mysterious presence, at once evoking wonder, filial fear, and a deeply rooted sense of security that nothing could shake. As has been widely noted, Our Lady of the Angels, a nearby church, began a joyful ringing of its bells as the young priest was flooded with a peace that would be further refined by decades of suffering for this new child of the Church born from the heart of God.

Opus Dei became a personal prelature of the Catholic Church in 1982, seven years after St. Josemaría was called to God. Though only forming a small portion of the Lord's vineyard, it nevertheless brings together in a lived synthesis many of the elements of the Morning Offering. In fact, in the spiritual practices that members of the Work follow, the very first is an offering of their day to God. Thus the Work's understanding of how to sanctify everyday life—of which work is an important feature—will help us put on the Lord's paten our works, our professions, and our vocations, those things we do daily that give expression to the talents and gifts we have been given by God.

For decades, Opus Dei has encouraged souls to do their work with the utmost human perfection so as to make a worthy offering to God. The teachings of St. Josemaría on doing our work in this way come down to four points: First, a person in love with God should flee superficiality. Therefore, a sense of responsibility should pervade all our efforts. More, we should hunger *to learn* how to work well, for it is "not enough to want to do good; we must know how to do it."[6] People in love are not careless or nonchalant when it comes to their beloved. The same holds for us when we offer our work to God.

Secondly, following the imperative from Leviticus 22:20 ("You shall not offer anything that has a blemish"), we seek to work with human excellence. We always work in the presence of our Father-God, and it is a constant desire of our heart to please him in all things. In those little, gritty details, in those moments when weariness sets in or our task seems either pointless or impossible, we redouble our efforts, renew our intentions, and out of love for our Creator offer him the very best we are capable of. We do this not to outdo others (that would be pride), to satisfy our desire for applause (that would be vanity), or to amass more material goods (that would be avarice) but to please our Father in heaven, who sees all things with his loving omniscience.

Thirdly, our efforts at a refined excellence in our work should stem from a sincere desire to serve the Lord and our neighbor. St. Josemaría wove this theme into a motto for our work, saying in a homily, "If you want to be useful, serve."[7] Lastly, we sanctify others through our work when we bring them closer to God. This essential dimension, a truly apostolic one, also provides us with a shield to fend off the temptations of pride, for we want not to be admired but to give witness to Christ by our human and supernatural authenticity.

In an anecdote St. Josemaría loved to repeat, the great cathedrals of Europe can teach much about offering our works to God:

> I used to enjoy climbing up the cathedral towers to get a close view of the ornamentation at the top, a veritable lacework of stone that must have been the result of very patient and laborious craftsmanship. As I chatted with the young men who accompanied me I used to point out that none of the beauty of this work could be seen from below. To give them a material lesson in what I had been previously explaining to them, I would say, "This is God's work, this is working for God! To finish your personal work perfectly, with all the beauty and exquisite refinement of this tracery stonework." Seeing it, my companions would understand that all the work we had seen was a prayer, a loving dialogue with God.[8]

The works we place on the paten of each day, of course, will not be as magnificent as that of a cathedral. Yet love of God must be woven in and through each of our works, regardless of whether they are of obvious importance to society, such as crafting the decision of a high court, explaining a crucial advance in medical technology, or just baking chocolate chip cookies for our children. Any good done for love of God, for souls, becomes a partaker of God's infinite love.

Wendell Berry, an American novelist and poet, has lived on the same farm in Kentucky for forty years. He knows about working out of love for the land as well as anyone does. In his lyric poem "Like Snow," he captures with perfect simplicity how we should work when inspired by a love human and divine:

> Suppose we did our work
> like the snow, quietly, quietly,
> leaving nothing out.[9]

5. Joys

Joy is the serious business of Heaven.

—C. S. Lewis, *Letters to Malcolm*

Why do we offer our joys to God? The question is worth asking because it reveals with greater clarity the reasons we offer anything to God. Yet before we answer that question, a larger issue looms.

Throughout the centuries, many have often seen our faith as something grim and, yes, joyless. Some of this is due to distortions of doctrine, some attributable to the failures and sins of individual Christians. As well, the misconceptions of nonbelievers often parody the faith and make it less compelling to the world, and seemingly without joy. Nonetheless, our faith does not destroy joy. Faith is rather the surest—indeed, only—path to real joy, and one that begins in this life, though it will only reach its fullness in the eternity of God. Christian joy is a foretaste of everlasting life, and the merest taste of that outweighs a world of counterfeit joys.

Pope Benedict XVI, in his first encyclical, *Deus Caritas Est*, asks a similar question about *eros*, romantic and sexual love: "Doesn't the Church, with all her commandments and prohibitions, turn to bitterness the most precious thing in life? Doesn't she blow the whistle just when the joy which is the Creator's gift offers us a happiness which is itself a certain foretaste of the Divine? But is this the case? Did Christianity really destroy *eros*?"[1]

His answer shows how the history of Christianity demonstrates the very opposite, that in fact both the Old and New Testaments "in no way" show "a war on eros as such" but actually a drive to destroy a "warped and destructive form of it."

Yet that warped form of eros—as well as other misused gifts and virtues—is rampant in our society: "The modern world is full of the old Christian virtues gone mad," as G. K. Chesterton put it.[2] We are living in an era where the reach of technology is nearly omnipresent. Social networks graft us onto a web from which escape is, by our own choosing, rare. Images of ever-improving technology, of opportunities for self-fulfillment, of lavish expenditure, of indulgence, and of depraved enjoyment wash over us in a tidal wave of seamless chatter. What do these images promise? They all promise, in varying degrees, joy.

Of course, the crucial questions are, how do we avoid the mirages of joy that delude so many? How do we find true joy?

God created this world good. All he does is good, and pleasure is his creation. Sin has disfigured this goodness, sometimes drastically, but the foundation of the whole cosmos is good because it comes from the hand of God (Ps 104:5). That, of course, does not mean everything unfolds with mechanistic necessity. God created Adam "in the power of his own inclination" (Sir 15:14), and therefore the drama of freedom marks creation with special splendors and shadows. And while tradition can hand on untold riches, each generation, each individual, must rediscover the ancient truths and make them flourish anew.

In the family, the interior landscape of the child, so to speak, is formed. While removing the guilt of original sin, God in his wisdom left within us the sting of concupiscence, that unruly tug of the passions for what is against reason and our true good. We must be aware that in a fallen world the best cannot be realized without suffering. There are moments of rest and refreshment, though, in which we can experience a foretaste of the joys that await us. These joys are given to us as solace, refreshment, and reminders of the bliss of heaven.

Friendship, based on a shared love for noble things— festive meals taken together with family, the beauty of nature (even that lovely but humble fragrance of freshly mown grass in the spring), the interior lifting of our heart that great literature or breathtaking art inspires, and the joy of successful endeavor that comes only after years of disciplined effort and dedicated prayer—is a gift meant to point to something more, something given to us in hope.

Why do many often miss this truth? Many believers see their faith as a burden, an obligation, anything but a source of joy. Perhaps many Catholics fail to "rejoice in the Lord" precisely because their misuse of natural joys impedes their enjoyment of supernatural ones (Phil 4:4).

For, as Aquinas put it, "No one can live without delight. This is why a man deprived of spiritual joy goes over to carnal pleasures."[3] As only rational beings are capable of joy, of *gaudium*, Aquinas firmly places the human person between the angels (capable of joy) and the animals (capable of only sensible pleasure, *delectatio*). Even our physical delights can accord with reason and thereby become worthy of the highest faculty within us. We are, in this sense, placed on a horizon between time and eternity, spirit and matter, and our cultivation of joy must reflect this basic reality about us.

To see the things of God—the reality of joy—to converse with him with the language of faith, one must love the truth enough to be willing to change our lives at its call, even to die for it, if necessary. The second-century writer Theophilus of Antioch put it this way: "God is perceived by men who are capable of seeing him, who have the eyes of their spirit open. Man's soul must be as pure as a shining mirror."[4] Such purity is difficult. Without grace, it isn't possible at all.

Yet in all our searching for joy, for happiness that is as full and as real as a sunrise, isn't there something else at play? Isn't there, when we think about it, the tang, the very taste, of the real? Not something dreamed about in a fantasy of desire or pride but something outside of us—friendship, love, beauty, and even sorrow when accepted in a supernatural spirit of trust—can awaken this joy within. In this sense, I must yearn in prayer for the maturity to accept these joys that come only in their own good time, after trial, effort, and patience, like manna from heaven—which indeed, all true joy is. In our heart of hearts, we know that all joy is based on the truth. And the truth, in all its fiery, personal transcendent glory, *is* Christ.

Now I can see that joy is something waited on, with reverence and calm, for it comes, ultimately, from Christ; in this life, even the tiniest joy is a hint, a shy shadow, of the unending bliss of seeing the Lord whose love, says Dante, moves the sun and the stars—and the hearts of saints, whose lot we so dearly pray to join in the fullness of eternal joy.

In this vision in heaven is the complete fulfillment of our humanity. Aquinas teaches us that even in this life the delights of the spirit are "absolutely" greater than the delights of the senses. He proves this by simply describing the activities of our intellect as more "intimate, more perfect, and more firm" than sensory delights. The object of bodily delights will pass away, but spiritual goods are everlasting.

Aquinas is not naive about the power of bodily pleasures. He knows they are more "vehement" than the spiritual delights because they move the body so strongly. Though we often seek bodily delights to counter bodily grief, the spiritual goods we enjoy have no "contrary." Nothing is contrary to God and the joys of his friendship in the sense that nothing competes with God. With Psalm 119, we can say, "How sweet are thy words to my taste, sweeter than honey to my mouth!" This is one reason C. S. Lewis wrote that joy is the serious business of heaven.

It is serious business because, really, it is the only business of heaven—the reason God, totally blessed and happy in himself, freely brought forth the cosmos and every soul that has ever lived, or will live.

This joy is a participation in the inner life of God, the ground of all that exists, and that life is one of perfect, ecstatic, self-gift, an eternal round of mutual giving, begotten, and proceeding bliss. This inner life is likened to a fire in scripture, one that purifies all it touches, which no one can see in this life and live. For to see this fire is to behold the face of God, and for that one must be divinized by grace down to the last whisker, as St. Josemaría Escrivá liked to say. But these hints we get here below—earthly prologues to an unending story of bliss—surpass every fleeting pleasure because they partake of the Holy Spirit's gifts which are meant for the eternity of joy which is heaven itself.

I offer this joy back to the Lord because it is the nature of joy to give with youthful exuberance that neither counts the cost nor holds back from fear.

St. Francis de Sales, writing in his *Treatise on the Love of God*, advised us to do this each day: "To make excellent progress in devotion, one must offer all one's actions to God every day, for by this daily renewal of our oblation we pour out upon our actions the vigor and virtue of tender love through a new application of our heart to the Divine Glory."[5]

So in our quiet offering of our day to the Lord, we see the greatest secret of the devout soul: its lasting, resilient, refined spiritual joy. Neither marred by sentimentality nor dependent on our moods, energy, good luck, or temperament, this joy is above all a gift of grace. Therefore a vital aspect of the Christian notion of joy is that it is an *effect* of God's life within us, an offshoot of friendship between God and the soul, a fruit of the virtue of charity.

I place my spiritual joy on the paten of this day's offering because the Holy Trinity is dwelling in my soul. This is the unmerited gift of sanctifying grace: "The kingdom of God does not mean food and drink but righteousness and peace and joy in the Holy Spirit" (Rom 14:17). Let our souls never forget, even as we are buoyed up by a joy not of this earth, that all grace and every gift from heaven—the sacraments that heal and sustain us along the journey of our life and the redemption itself—come at the price of the Cross.

What originates from a miracle, such as the wine of Cana, is far finer than what comes from nature. Our Lord's Passion was greater than any other human suffering possible. His sacred humanity was miraculously formed in the immaculate womb of Our Lady by the Holy Spirit. The sensitivity of his body felt the blows and the lash with unimaginable pain, while his soul, filled with every grace and virtue, endured the sorrow arising from the betrayal, rejection, mockery, hate, scorn, and indifference that wounded him from every side.

The light of Easter morning must not forget the shadows of Good Friday. The roots of Christian joy are indeed in the shape of a cross.[6] They run deep into the heart of God, who was wounded for sin and is now triumphantly risen, offering us a joy no one can take from us (Jn 16:22).

This joy is so vast that it does not so much enter into us as we enter into it. Our joy in heaven is a creaturely participation by grace in God's very joy of himself. So we come into this joy much as we might step into the audience hall of a great king. Except this is the Lord of lords, and he has waited from before the ages to welcome us into something better than any palace, the heart of God.

"Enter into the joy of your master" (Mt 25:21).

6. Sufferings

No cross is so extreme, as to have none.

—John Donne

Suffering is part of every life, a truth obvious to everyone. We enter this world, after all, howling for nourishment, warmth, affection, and nearly everything else. Our early growth depends on internalizing certain priorities, controlling urges, and learning by repeated, painful steps to become independent of our parents.

As we grow, the extent to which we will nourish our gifts will depend, in large part, on how well we have deferred our impulses and the boisterous appetites within us, clamoring for satisfaction. Just being able to read the morning paper, drive to work, and engage well one's profession requires more self-denial than we realize. Seeing suffering as the worst evil in our life overlooks how every human growth involves some sacrifice, some denial, and some dying. Only a culture sunk in adolescent illusion denies this truth.

Without the grace of Christ, I can be as cowardly as anyone in the face of this darkly lit mystery. Yet the day we banish all suffering in our lives might be the day we lose sight of the last trace of ourselves as created in the image of God. Even so, the blessings of science and medicine are to be

41

used with gratitude, for suffering is not from God but from humanity's abuse of the gift of freedom.

Moral evil, to be sure, is a scandal. The monstrous evil done over the centuries, often by Christians, is one of the most potent hindrances to belief in God. Though the false gods of ideology in the last century have created the greatest bloodletting the world has ever seen, the sins of Catholics are enough to remind us how much the face of Christ's Church is often disfigured by malice, unspeakable infidelity, widespread indifference, and worldliness. That is why Aquinas writes, in his *Commentary on the Book of Job*, "Nothing appears to impugn divine providence in human affairs more than the affliction of the innocent."[1] Of course, the key word there is "appears." For in truth, there is one mystery in this world greater than the mystery of evil, and that is the mystery of Christ's love for his wayward creation.

The Christian knows that all suffering is the result of sin.

Not all suffering is the result of personal sin, it is true (see Christ's curing of the man blind from birth, Jn 9:1–41). But the world of suffering, of death, and of the myriad evils of life has all come from humanity's original sin and our own actual sins. Only good can come from God's hand, nothing else. The greatest evil, therefore, is not suffering but offending God, the loving source of every good.

When we set ourselves up as the arbiter of right and wrong ("You will be like God" [Gn 3:5]), we misuse the gift of intelligence in a self-justifying act of spiritual arrogance. The rebellion of our first parents left us without grace, without the preternatural gifts that kept their bodies perfectly attuned to their will, which was fully oriented toward God's will, their hearts resting in his heart. When they disobeyed a perfectly reasonable command—trust the God they spoke with in the garden during the cool of the day (Gn 3:8)—the harmony they experienced as his gift was lost. Their wills having rebelled, their bodies followed: their appetites lost their supernatural orientation, and the human race became unruly, wild as an unbridled horse.

According to the poet John Milton, the moment Eve ate the fruit, "earth felt the wound."[2] That wound cuts deeply into the human heart. We feel it when our own hour of death approaches but also when a loved one dies. We feel the wound when someone close to us is far from God and when we are lied to, manipulated, betrayed, ill, depressed, and misunderstood. We feel the wound when we see the faith either despised or distorted, or both—or when, as did St. Paul, we feel the unruly "old man" within us, pulling in the opposite direction from where we know we should go. When we see the sins of Catholics—ourselves included—disfiguring the Bride of Christ, becoming a scandal to others, and when we see how marred by ignorance and sin this poor world is, we suffer.

This is the suffering we must offer to God each day.

This is the suffering that only the human person can experience, and as such it is a thread woven throughout our life but one now made golden by the very hand of the suffering Christ. He has taken all this poverty unto himself, so that "all flesh shall see the salvation of God" (Lk 3:6). We must pray, not so much that we don't suffer, but that we do the right and holy thing with the suffering that comes our way by God's fatherly providence.

Here are a few ways of making our offering of this precious suffering a little easier, a little lighter on our hearts: In times of suffering, we must recall that God knows we are made of dust (Gn 3:19); he knows how easily the burdens of our fallen nature weigh on us. Here, in suffering, prayer is purified; the heart is turned inside out and pressed close to the Cross, and all superfluities, all illusions, and all self-clinging are drawn from the souls God labors to bring to himself.

In such moments, we need to see before us the dream of God, what he has planned before all ages. From his infinite fullness of his being, God has willed from all eternity to give us through Christ adoption as his children, his very sons and daughters. He does this not to complete his own happiness—which is infinitely perfect and therefore in need of nothing—but to complete our happiness by sharing in his intimate life, the life of grace, as we call it.

We are drawn, after all, from nothingness. Yet we occasionally hear some say that our God is a suffering God, "who suffers with his creatures." This is founded on an erroneous idea of God. We must not consider this ruin that has come into our world as God's fault, or as a sign of some imperfection of his. As Dom Columba Marmion reminds us, he is infinitely perfect, infinitely blessed entirely in himself. He does not need anything, let alone us, to complete his perfections. In fact, from all eternity, he has known the result of our misused freedoms.

Father Thomas G. Weinandy, writing on the question of God suffering with us, makes this observation: "The importance of God's immanent activity is predicated in direct proportion to His transcendence. It is precisely because God transcends the whole created order of time and history that His immanent actions within time and history acquire singular significance."[3]

While it may sound emotionally satisfying to say that God suffers with us, if "God is in as much trouble as we are," no help for suffering or pain exists. Our entire Tradition—revelation and sound philosophy—has shown that God in his divinity dwells in a different order of existence than his creation. His ability to console, heal, and transform us in our afflictions is infinite.

His mercy can then reach down into the deepest spiritual pain precisely because he is the Lord of being, the God "who give life to the dead and call into existence the things that do not exist" (Rom 4:17). Because his ways are not our ways (Is 55:8), he can bring us out of our misery into his perfect, unending bliss.

He does this, of course, precisely in the suffering and death of Jesus. The Incarnation is itself an icon of God's desire to be with us, to suffer with us, and to take upon himself our sin and death and transform them into life. Benedict XVI, in the first volume of *Jesus of Nazareth*, finds this same motif of divine sympathy for humanity running through all of Christ's words and deeds. This solidarity for his creation—promised in Genesis—begins definitively anew in the Baptism of the Lord: "Looking at the events in the light of the Cross and Resurrection, the Christian people realized what happened: Jesus loaded the burden of all of mankind's guilt upon his shoulders; he bore it down into the depths of the Jordan. He inaugurated his public activity by stepping into the place of sinners."[4] The divine Son is also the Son of Man. He is the inextinguishable light that can burn away the darkness of our sin, his Baptism so pure that even death must give way (Lk 12:49).

Anyone who thinks Christians are either grim-faced pessimists or impractical idealists should read the verbal diptych found in book twenty-two of St. Augustine's *On the City of God*. Here Augustine shows forth on one hand the evils of life that cause us suffering: griefs, fears, strife, war, pride, envy, ambition, lust, cruelty, murder, ignorance, folly, storms, landslides, poisoned fruits and water, biting horses (one of the many hazards, I suppose, of traveling in the fifth century), famine, illnesses of mind and body, medical cures that are worse than the illness, demons, nightmares, hunger, and thirst.

The list is long, and though the details have changed, it's not unlike life today, especially if one takes a perspective beyond the developed world. Ironically, countries with the most material goods are often beset by psychological sufferings, many quite acute, despite great advances in pharmacological treatment for depression and anxiety, for instance. Anyone who has ever suffered from a mental illness, or has someone close to them that has, knows how this affliction of the mind and spirit is a heavy cross.

Augustine ends his depiction of the sorrows of life with the thought that grace is meant not to help us to escape our sufferings but to help us "bear them with a stout heart."[5] Augustine, as with Columba Marmion, never loses sight of the "real purpose of religion," which is the "felicity of that other life in which all our ills will be no more."[6]

The list of the blessings of God showers on us in this life, the second panel in the diptych, as it were, is amazing. Here Augustine certainly gives the lie to the Enlightenment stereotype of the divide between Renaissance humanists who celebrated humanity and the early pessimistic Augustine, harbinger of the so-called Dark Ages. Of course, even in his description of the ills of life, Augustine doesn't come close to despairing. Yet in his description of the blessings of life, he virtually breaks out into song!

The first of these blessings is the gift of procreation, life-giving powers woven throughout creation. This gift finds a special crowning in humanity, for the "inbreathing of the soul" shows God's intimate creative act bringing each person into the world, fulfilling in a most splendid manner how he "is working still" (Jn 5:17). This human ability to engage in reasoning and intellection gives us "a divinely given capacity for goods so high that this marvel is beyond any tongue to express or mind to comprehend."[7] From this font—the human soul—Augustine traces out the myriad wonders of this fallen yet beautiful world.

Augustine's pen paints a portrait of humanity's unique achievements: our crafts, paintings, and sculptures; our cooking with uncountable spices, herbs, and relishes; our dramas, with their poetry, rhetoric, and song; our politics, mathematics, and philosophical inquiries; our medicines; our devices used in war; our architecture; our agriculture; and our navigation of the seas and oceans. All these things make the "human mind . . . a glory of this mortal life."[8]

After detailing these riches of our intellect, Augustine extols the human body, "a revelation of the goodness of God."[9] Our appearance, form, and stature all minister to the gift of our intellectual, spiritual nature as we "walk erect" with "eyes on things above," rather than rooting around on the ground as irrational animals do.[10] Indeed, the "rhythm, poise, and symmetry" of our bodies make Augustine wonder whether the Creator had utility or beauty most in mind when he created us.[11] The profound organization of the human person, externally as well as internally, bring to his mind the "*harmonia*" of the Greeks, a "rhythm of relationships" that weave form and function into an organic whole that is wonderful to contemplate.[12]

This spiritual ordering of the parts into a single being, if we could perfectly understand it, would reveal to the mind "so ravishing a beauty that no visible shapeliness of form that delights the eye . . . could be compared with it."[13] I have dwelled a moment on St. Augustine's twin portrait of the woes and blessing of our life to underscore some important realities: Unlike some of the Reformers of the sixteenth century, we do not believe in a doctrine of "total depravity," wherein the human person is thoroughly corrupted and unable to do anything according to its nature. As Augustine wrote in the same chapter of *The City of God*, "The penalties imposed do not mean the total deprivation of all that God has given."[14]

Moreover, the Redeemer of this flawed yet still magnificent human person actually is *he who made us, and he who made everything that exists, the cosmos itself.* Our Redeemer is God the Father's only Son—the eternal Word of God, expressing eternally, and infinitely, the Father's own essence and utterance: "All things were made through him" (Jn 1:3).

The Passion of Our Lord becomes the underlying hope of every suffering borne out of a love of God and neighbor. This is not something that belongs merely to history: the sacrifice of the Mass is the renewal of Christ's luminous triumph over death. The Word through which all things were made is the Son through whom all things are healed and brought to God.

To the eyes of faith, all things reveal this exquisite, tender love of God, who is Creator and Redeemer.

Evil, therefore, has not won, nor has it ripped a hole in the ground of being. The senselessness and the absurdity of evil, the willfulness of it, its love of negation, and its fondness for an ironical posturing of the good has all ultimately lost and been swallowed up in the descent of God into our darkness wherein his light cannot be overshadowed (Jn 1:5). The sufferings of Christ take the worst that sin can deliver and nails it to the Cross, that new tree of life of which we are now invited to partake. We can join St. Paul in his triumphant cry: "O death, where is thy victory? O death, where is thy sting?" (1 Cor 15:55).

We know from the saints that suffering becomes redemptive—that is, an offering in reparation for sin—when joined to the Cross. Not all suffering partakes of the Holy Cross, of course. Perhaps there is no greater tragedy in life than to suffer without belief in the redemptive treasures found in the Cross. If only we join our wills in faith to the sacrifice of Calvary, no pain or suffering is beyond redemption. Yet without faith, how will we know this?

Suffering when joined to the Cross has another purpose: suffering can purify us. For who among us can say he or she does not need purification? Our Church identifies sufferings, both voluntary and those that providence allows or wills into our life, as a tremendous means to purify our souls from sin, selfishness, unbelief, evil habits, and most of all, a lack of charity.

For, if we are honest, we know we would not purify ourselves without these trials. As the great Abbot Blosius wrote, "Nothing more valuable can befall a man than tribulation, when it is endured with patience for the love of God; because there is no more certain sign of the divine election."[15]

In this way, inner joys can also exist alongside suffering and sorrow, as photographs of the saints of the last century and a half eloquently give witness.

7. *T*his Day

*"I wish it need not have happened in my time," said Frodo.
"So do I," said Gandalf, "and so do all who live to see
such times. But that is not for them to decide. All we have
to decide is what to do with the time that is given us."*
—J. R. R. Tolkien, *The Fellowship of the Ring*

Whether our days be ordinary or, as with Frodo, filled with extraordinary hardships in which the fate of many souls depend on how well we hold up, the day, this day, "the time" we have, is a gift. It may not seem so. But Christianity has never claimed to remove suffering from our midst—quite the contrary. Our Lord himself set the requirements for being his disciple, with no wiggle room: "And he who does not take his cross and follow me is not worthy of me" (Mt 10:38).

In much of the developed world, daily life has become largely secularized in negative ways, making little room for God, thereby unraveling, as it were, the tapestry of each moment—rich with the divine presence—so that hours become not gift but tedium, not opportunity but something to be borne only with medication to help us sleep, work, or do whatever it is we are supposed to do. In a way, this battle with ennui is as dangerous as any horde of orcs Frodo faced to save his lovely shire.

We have plenty of things beyond ennui, of course, to worry about. In the West, we are suffering under what Benedict XVI called the "dictatorship of relativism." Abortion, the greatest shroud darkening the conscience of our world today, is often tied to foreign aid to developing countries. The Guttmacher Institute reports that in 2008 there were approximately 43,800,000 abortions worldwide.[1] In 2012, out-of-wedlock births in the United States skyrocketed past the 40 percent mark, greatly increasing the number of children living in poverty, both material and spiritual.[2] The legally mandated splintering of the traditional family, based on false notions of equality and human happiness where one's will becomes the only norm by which to guide one's actions, makes a mockery of the common good. In all of this, we do violence to the weakest among us, and the dignity of our being made in the image of God is obscured by a moral darkness that is as deadly as it is pervasive.

Behind these numbers and trends lies immense suffering and countless offenses that cry to heaven. So as we consider how to live this day as an offering to Our Lord, we must try to see these shadows and sorrows in the light of the Cross and in the light of faith that tells us of God's infinite goodness and his ability to triumph over even immense evil. We must take to heart the bedrock truth that "God did not make death" (Wis 1:13). We must reflect on how close to us God is and, indeed, how "in him we live and move and have our being" (Acts 17:28). This is difficult sometimes but vital if we are to live in the reality in which God has placed us.

In our own life, we may be filled with great joy and thanksgiving, or conversely, we may be mourning the death of a loved one; suffering from a long-standing illness; or plagued with persistent unemployment, loneliness, spiritual aridity, a loss of faith, divisions in our family life or marriage, separation, divorce, or the long agony of seeing our children abandon the Faith that our parents so lovingly handed on to us. How are we to offer *this day* to God when all we have is touched by suffering—or, if we are more fortunate, when all we have could be lost in a moment? Our happiness in this life, it seems, is such a fragile thing, our days held together by a string as flimsy as a child's kite and apparently just as durable.

A traditional way of dealing with life's sorrows goes back to the gospels for its original inspiration. This is called the life of abandonment to divine providence. It is rooted in the humble image from Christ's exhortation to live each moment with absolute trust in God's fatherly care: "Are not two sparrows sold for a penny? And not one of them will fall to the ground without your Father's will. But even the hairs of your head are all numbered. Fear not, therefore; you are of more value than many sparrows" (Mt 10:29–31). Christ gives this exhortation after calling the Twelve and assigning them their apostolic mission, which will see persecution, betrayal from within, and except for John, the shedding of their blood for the Gospel's sake.

This way or spirituality is far from a "don't worry" attitude toward life, for Christ shares with his disciples—his friends—what he himself knows perfectly: the intimacy of God the Father's providential presence.

In the mystical tradition of the Church, two names stand prominently before us in this regard: St. Francis de Sales and Father Jean-Pierre de Caussade. St. Francis de Sales, a bishop and doctor of the Church, finished his *Introduction to the Devout Life* in 1609. Originally in the form of letters to a noble woman, this work was translated into numerous languages and has found a receptive readership ever since its first publication. It has rightly been judged a masterpiece of spiritual direction by lay, clerical, and religious readers. Its major emphasis concerns how to develop trust in the providence of God by preserving at all costs an interior peace born of that trust.

St. Francis shows a wise assessment of the dangers of anxiety: "With the single exception of sin, anxiety is the

greatest evil that can happen to a soul."[3] This is so not because
a placid state of being is desired before all else but because
of the self-love, distrust, and lack of supernatural faith often
behind our anxious hearts. The devout soul waits on the
Lord, doing all with the strength of holy meekness. Before
such a heart, trials come and go, but its attachment to the
Lord never wavers. Through the crucible of trial it has learned
this profound truth: "Abandonment is the virtue of virtues;
it is the cream of charity, the fragrance of humility, and the
fruit of perseverance."[4]

The work usually attributed to Caussade, *Abandonment
to Divine Providence*, published in 1861, is the classic work
of this spirituality. Little is known about Father Caussade
other than his quiet ministry for the Jesuits in cities such as
Champagne and Nancy. He died in Toulouse in 1751. The first
editor of *L'Abandon à la providence divine* was Father Henri
Ramiere who was a director of the Apostleship of Prayer
mentioned in our introduction. Ramiere obtained the manuscript from a convent of the Sisters of Nazareth of Montmirail,
sixty miles north of Paris.

The spirituality of abandonment to divine providence
is simple and yet profoundly aware of God's intimate presence. This work can transform our lives, if only we heed its
quiet teaching that sheds marvelous light on everyday life.
Father Caussade lays down a basic ground rule: this work
eschews all "method" by which we would automatically
attain a friendship with God. Christianity doesn't work like
that, and so neither does a spirituality that claims to take as
its inspiration and goal the Word Incarnate, Jesus Christ.

In any growth in our abandonment to God's providence,
God himself is the protagonist, not ourselves: "The doctrine
concerning pure love can only be taught by the action of God,
and not by any effort of the mind. God teaches the soul by
pains and obstacles, not by ideas."[5] This purity of heart is
a lifelong endeavor, brought about by grace and "constant
crosses, and a long succession of mortifications, trials, and

deprivations."[6] No method, then, but the Cross and the infinite graces that flow from it.

Caussade then describes the spiritual lives of those long ago, before there was "any regular method of spiritual direction." While regarding direction as necessary in our age, it is important for us to realize, he tells us, that for the Patriarchs, the holy men and women of the old covenant, Our Lady, her spouse St. Joseph, and countless others, known in scripture or known only to God, guidance largely came to them informally, but illuminated by great faith. These "hidden springs" of faith most notably motivated Our Lady. She was the simplest of creatures yet the closest to God: "Her answer to the angel when she said: '*Fiat mihi secundam verbum tuum*' ('Let it be to me according to your word' [Lk 1:38]) contained all the mystic theology of her ancestors to whom everything was reduced, as it is now, to the purest, simplest submission of the soul to the will of God, under whatever form it presents itself."[7]

This simplicity is a result of a profound theological insight: the omnipresence of God. Even so, our vision—so intimate to who we are, for the manner of our seeing is shaped by who we are before God—is not always to be trusted. We think we see all that is before us, but in reality we often see life in a superficial manner, however sophisticated we may think we are. According to de Caussade, we must acknowledge how much we need the gift of faith: "We live according to what we see and feel and wander like madmen in a labyrinth of darkness and illusion for want of the light of faith that would guide us safely through it."[8]

Yet were we to see as the Patriarchs of old saw, or with the eyes of the saints, we would realize something amazing:

> All creatures that exist are in the hands of God. The action of the creature can only be perceived by the senses, but faith sees in all things the action of the Creator. It believes that in Jesus Christ all things live, and that His divine

> operation continues to the end of time, embracing the
> passing moment and the smallest created atom in its hid-
> den life and mysterious action. There is not a moment
> in which God does not present Himself under the cover
> of some pain to be endured, of some consolation to be
> enjoyed, or of some duty to be performed. All that takes
> place within us, around us, or through us, contains and
> conceals His divine action.[9]

Why would God do this? Why would he come to us in
such disguise? Much has to do with the purity of his infinite
divine being, which is beyond all categories, forms, modes, or
genus. "Man shall not see me and live" (Ex 33:20). This Moses
heard from the fiery bush that was lit with unquenchable
fire, consuming yet unconsumed beyond all ages. This is the
God in whom we should believe and trust without measure.

Caussade also tells us, "So God hides Himself in order
to raise souls up to that perfect faith which will discover Him
under every kind of disguise."[10] Why does he want to raise
us to this level of faith, beyond our nature, and painful to the
Adam in us that would prefer something we could see, touch,
imagine, or at least schedule?

Once again we must meditate and make our own the
Church's teaching on the supernatural destiny of the human
person. What is the plan of God in his revelation in Christ,
in founding a Church, or in instituting a sacramental system
of worship founded on his sacrificial offering on Calvary?
In his *Summa Theologiae*, Thomas Aquinas asks if the created
intellect needs any "created light" in order to see the essence
of God. His answer is yes, we need what is called the "*lumen
gloriae*": the light of glory, a "supernatural disposition," and
a strengthening and illumination of the intellect so that the
very essence of God becomes visible to us in heaven. It is by
this light that "the blessed are made *deiform*, that is, like to
God."[11] Thomas quotes St. John: "When he appears we shall
be like to him, for we shall see him as he is" (1 Jn 3:2). In this
we have the highest understanding of the Christian destiny

of humanity: we are to see God by God and live in him by his very life.

Caussade strikes a similar note but with his emphasis on simplicity: "The designs of God, the good pleasure of God, the will of God, the operation of God, and the gift of His grace are all one and the same thing in the spiritual life. It is God working in the soul to make it like unto Himself."[12] His teaching frequently encourages us to drink deeply of these truths, or they will do us no good. Indeed, Caussade displays at times a certain wariness of the kind of speculation that leaves divine truth in a book, rather than imprinted on the heart by actually living those truths: "When one is thirsty, one quenches one's thirst by drinking, not by reading books which treat of this condition."[13] Nevertheless, the warning here is not to forgo the depths of theological truth but to ensure that we partake of those truths in our actual day-to-day living.

Here we see the reason that in the Eastern Churches, the Apostle John is known as "the Theologian." He is so by his intimacy with Our Lord in prayer, in friendship, and now in eternal glory. His knowledge (intellect), prayer (heart), and life (will) were all transformed by supernatural charity, *caritas*, burned clean by the light that comes into the world in the face of Christ. John's knowledge was transfigured by love, and in this way his love gave voice to the deepest wellsprings of grace and theological wisdom.

If we seek his face, we must study our faith, and we must read sacred scripture, especially the gospels. We must seek out wise spiritual direction, and most of all, we must partake of the Blessed Sacrament at Holy Mass, with time before the tabernacle. We must never forget to live the ordinary moments of *this day* in the presence of Christ, who is so close that he hears the beating of our heart.

This is the spirit with which we should make our Morning Offering. So holy is each moment of this day that de Caussade breaks out into an ecstatic series of metaphors:

"What treasures of grace lie concealed in this moments, filled, apparently, by the most ordinary events. . . . O Bread of Angels! heavenly manna! pearl of the Gospel! Sacrament of the present moment! thou givest God under as lowly a form as the manger, the hay, or the straw. And to whom doest thou give Him? 'He gives the hungry all good things.'"[14] In the sacrament of the present moment, God truly does give himself to the poor. Here Caussade is most attentive to the workings of the Holy Spirit "who arranges all the pieces on the board of life." Indeed, writes Caussade, at the moment a soul abandons himself or herself to God, the Holy Spirit will say, "*Fiat lux!*" Then God reveals himself and "all that is common becomes wonderful in itself, a miracle, a revelation, a constant joy."[15]

This "abyss of peace and contentment with God" is itself a foretaste of the Sabbath of eternity. Regardless of whether our day holds within its hands the fate of many or if our life's work is ordinary, the message of the Gospel is that no destiny is ordinary, and there is no moment that cannot be offered to the heart of God.

The isolation, alienation, and loneliness that so many feel today—ironically so, in this wired world of ours—can only be made whole and healed by a tender, intimate friendship with the Risen One, who died a horrific death so that every soul may dwell in peace with him in heaven.

We see each day as it unfolds moment by moment, yet God, in his infinite perfection and bliss, sees all. Aquinas has drawn a remarkable image of this divine vision, one that should help us make our Morning Offering in utter confidence: "With like certitude God knows, in his eternity, all that takes place throughout the whole course of time. For his eternity is in present contact with the whole course of time, and even passes beyond time. We may fancy that God knows the flight of time in his eternity, in the way that a person standing on top of a watchtower embraces in a single glance a whole caravan of passing travelers."[16] How marvelous is this image! What comfort it should give us. He knows our prayer before we give it breath (both his gifts) and has accepted our Morning Offering from before the world began.

In one of his lyrical meditations from the point of view of God the Father, French poet Charles Péguy finds the perfect image for this abandonment that brings the peace the world cannot give: "The man who is in my hand like the staff in the traveler's hand, that man is acceptable to me, says God."[17]

Whole treasures of grace lie in this image.

8. $\mathcal{S}$acred Heart

Personally I find perfection quite easy to practice because I have realized that all one has to do is take Jesus by the heart.

—St. Thérèse of Lisieux

Thanks partly to the writings of Pope Benedict XVI, we know that there was a false dichotomy that became popular after the Second Vatican Council. This trend pitted participation in the liturgy against devotions such as the Rosary and devotion to the Sacred Heart of Jesus. After half a century, we can see now that this posed an erroneous alternative for the faithful and that active participation in the liturgy is not in any intrinsic way threatened by private practices of piety, many of those founded by saints.

In fact, the interiority gained in these devotions is an essential contribution to the liturgical life of Catholics. According to Benedict, "The liturgy itself can only be celebrated properly if it is prepared for, and accompanied by, that meditative 'abiding' in which the heart begins to see and to understand, drawing the senses too into its beholding."[1]

Father Henri Ramière saw in the early years of the Apostleship of Prayer how the Sacred Heart of Jesus is vital to our Morning Offering. The basis of this devotion is the reality of the Incarnation. For instance, in the Councils of

Nicaea (AD 325) and Chalcedon (AD 451), faith in the person of Christ as fully human and fully divine is taught, in the words of St. Athanasius, as the "original . . . teaching and faith of the Catholic Church, which the Lord bestowed, the Apostles proclaimed, and the Fathers safeguarded."[2]

Pope Leo I, writing to a bishop during the Council of Chalcedon, put this doctrine so succinctly that the council Fathers had his letter entered into the council documents. He wrote, "As the Word does not lose its glory which is equal to that of the Father, so neither does the flesh leave the nature of its kind behind. . . . A lowly cradle manifests the infancy of the child; angels' voices announce the greatness of the most High."[3]

While it is true that specific attention paid to Our Lord's heart as an object of worship and devotion did not flower until the Middle Ages, there are roots to this practice that run deep into the foundations of Christianity's earliest years.

In John's gospel, we read an eyewitness account of the final hours of Jesus on the cross. John's knowledge of the scriptures helps us see how our redemption was foreseen centuries before by prophecy:

> But when they came to Jesus and saw that he was already dead, they did not break his legs. But one of the soldiers pierced his side with a spear, and at once there came out blood and water. He who saw it has borne witness—his testimony is true, and he knows that he tells the truth—that you also may [come to] believe. For these things took place that the scripture might be fulfilled: "Not a bone of him shall be broken." And again another scripture says, "They shall look on him whom they have pierced." (Jn 19:33–37)

That the bones of Jesus were not broken reveals him as the lamb of the true and definitive Passover (Ex 12:46). The second citation, from Zechariah 12:10, is an apocalyptic reference to the sorrows of Jerusalem leading mysteriously to its ultimate triumph. St. Bonaventure, writing in the twelfth century, sees this event as an eruption of divine love into the world: "The blood and water which poured out at that moment were the price of our salvation. Flowing from the secret abyss of Our Lord's heart as from a fountain, this stream gave the sacraments of the Church the power to confer the life of grace, while for those already living in Christ it became a spring of living water welling up to life everlasting."[4]

St. Bonaventure is an important source for the development of this devotion because he sees the Sacred Heart as the portal through which the currents of God's grace flow into his Church and the world. Aquinas thought as much when he wrote that the water and the blood flowing from Christ's side signify Baptism and Eucharist, the gateway and the summit, respectively, of our sacramental life.

How fitting it is that the youthful, pure heart of St. John would witness this event. His heart beat in time with the heart of Our Lord before Good Friday, and it is this sympathy, this relationship born of truth and fidelity, that renders him worthy of seeing the heart of Jesus in the extremity of "loving to the end" the world he had fashioned from eternity.

This passage of John's gospel gives us a unique insight into Christ's death and its meaning for the world. In the Vulgate translation, the Latin word *continuo* means "immediately," but it also means "continuously," which well describes the constant outpouring of sacramental graces flowing from the sacrifice of Calvary. It also bears witness to the centuries of interior life springing, as Bonaventure wrote, from this source, the heart of Christ. Those who believe the Church should not change from its earliest decades misunderstand the nature of organic growth. The deposit of faith given to the apostles cannot change. It can, however, grow in depth and explicit clarity in the life of the Church. We must remember something easily forgotten in the culture of vulgarity that often reigns in our time: whatever is sacred and whatever is holy should be veiled in silence until the right moment calls for disclosure by a loving heart.

Devotion to the Sacred Heart of Jesus has grown out of such a contemplative silence in the Church. Reverence for God's sovereign freedom, in fact, plays a major part in recognizing these new depths of spirituality. In this light, we find growing over the long centuries an emphasis on the heart of the Redeemer. St. Justin Martyr, St. Augustine, St. John Chrysostom, and others explored the human heart in its passionate seeking for God and God's answer in Christ's own Passion.

While medieval writers such as St. Anselm, St. Bernard, St. Gertrude, St. Mechtilde, and later, St. Francis de Sales and St. John Eudes have written on the Sacred Heart and can be said to have developed its essential dimensions based on their prayerful reading of scripture, without doubt St. Margaret Mary Alacoque is the preeminent source for the modern form of this devotion. With such distinguished predecessors, however, is it any wonder that the popes who approved devotion to the Sacred Heart stated that they were not basing this practice on a single person so much as disseminating a treasure that Our Lord himself cultivated from the rich depths of the Church's interior life?

Yet in an obscure convent in an obscure corner of seventeenth-century France, Christ did reveal to a single soul a specific appeal by which humanity may have renewed access to his infinite mercy. This access, as with many things of God, came by means of an image, amid an atmosphere of suffering, self-abnegation, prayer, misunderstanding, endless self-giving, mortification, solitude, loneliness, and an often overlooked but indescribable peace.

In other words, it grew in the shadow of the Cross.

The outward details are fairly simple. Margaret Alacoque was born on July 22, 1647, in a tiny town of Burgundy, the fifth of seven children. Her father was a prosperous notary, with holdings in the country. He died when she was around eight years old, sending the family's finances into chaos. For several years, relatives ruled the house, treating her mother and the children as servants. When her oldest brother reached legal maturity, the family regained its financial and emotional stability. After a brief search for the right convent, Margaret, having disavowed marriage, chose the Order of the Visitation, founded by St. Francis de Sales, at Paray-le-Monial.

Taking the name of Mary, she helped in the infirmary and quietly cultivated her love of mental prayer and intense devotion to Our Lord's presence in the tabernacle. Starting in December 1673, she began to have a series of mystical experiences in which Christ was calling her to a deeper level of self-denial than she deemed possible. At one point, she spent an evening resting on Our Lord's chest, listening, as did St. John, to the beating of his heart.

In June 1675, sometime after Easter, St. Margaret Mary received the task that Christ had given to her for the entire Church. In some form, whether interior locution or apparition, Christ told her to abandon all to him: "I was to cling to nothing, to empty and despoil myself of everything, to love nothing but Him, in him, and for the love of Him, to see all things naught from but Him and the interests of His glory in complete forgetfulness of myself."[5]

One day before the Blessed Sacrament, during the Octave of Corpus Christi, wishing to return to the Lord some token of his love, she was shown something few mortals see in this life. Our Lord said to her,

> Behold this heart, which has loved men so much, that It has spared Itself nothing, even to exhausting and consuming Itself, in order to testify to them Its love; and in return I receive from the greater number nothing but ingratitude and contempt which they show me in this sacrament of love. But what I feel most keenly is that hearts which are consecrated to Me that treat me thus. Therefore, I ask of thee that the Friday after the Octave of Corpus Christi be set apart for a special Feast to honor

My Heart, by communicating on that day and making
reparation to It by a solemn act, in order to make amends
for the indignities which It has received during the time
It has been exposed on the altars.[6]

At the request of her superior, St. Margaret Mary wrote a
short spiritual autobiography. It is a sobering read. Her life of
forty-three years—she died in 1690—was marked by tremendous sufferings, bodily and spiritual. Yet amid such crosses
as being bedridden for four years and continual spiritual
agonies that paralleled Our Lord's desolation in Gethsemane
and agony on the cross, she wrote in all simplicity, "My heart
. . . was always in a state of unalterable peace."[7] After Father
Claude de Colombiere, a Jesuit, became her spiritual director
at the convent, she at least had someone who believed her
experiences were genuinely supernatural. Devotion to the
Sacred Heart was not new to the Church, but Our Lord's
request for a "special Feast," with consecration and reparation at the center of it, was.

Within seventy-five years of her death, the Holy See
approved devotion to the Sacred Heart in the form commu-
nicated to St. Margaret Mary. In March 1824, Pope Leo XII
declared her venerable; in September 1864, Pius IX beatified
her; and she was canonized by Benedict XV in 1920. Father
Colombière, her spiritual advisor, after a dramatic career in
the Court of St. James, returned to France two years before
his death in 1682, where he often rested at Paray-le-Monial,
and could further advise this sister who was such a humble
recipient of extraordinary graces. John Paul II canonized him
in 1992.

We offer the Lord our day for "all the intentions" of his
"Sacred Heart." What are those intentions? According to the
life of St. Margaret Mary Alacoque, and confirmed by the
teaching of the Church, they are several in number but all
have to do with our sanctification, with our becoming holy
because he is holy (Lv 11:44). How are we to do this? We must

remember that St. Margaret Mary's memoir, bracing as it is in the account of the sufferings of her life, is essentially a love song to Our Lord. While her vocation to leave the world has unique features, the spousal, covenanted love between her soul and Christ is a lofty and pristine example of the tender love that should exist between every soul and the Lord.

While varieties of sensibility, specific to men and women, the married or those in the single life, or priestly vocation, will change some details of the expression of this devotion, the essential core of it remains unchanged. In the revelation of this devotion to the Sacred Heart of Jesus, we see, in all its intimacy and fineness of spirit, the Lord God as the lover of souls: "How can I give you up, O E'phraim? How can I hand you over, O Israel? . . . My heart recoils within me, my compassion grows warm and tender" (Hos 11:8).

This metaphorical expression of God's love in the Old Testament, as Benedict XVI has noted, now becomes literal in the heart of Christ: "Incarnational spirituality must be a spirituality of the passions, a spirituality of 'heart to heart'; in that way, precisely, it is an Easter spirituality, for the mystery of Easter, the mystery of suffering, is of its very nature a mystery of the heart."[9] For the Christian, "the way" is the sacred humanity of Christ and, preeminently, his Sacred Heart.

One only needs a brief acquaintance with the gospels to see how essential the purification of the heart is to Christian discipleship. St. Margaret Mary avails herself of this purification with tenacity. A reader today may easily overlook in the at times delicate emotional tenor of her autobiography her steely will forged in suffering. Her love of Christ and souls (and especially the poor, for whom she had a deep compassion) and her willingness to suffer in reparation for sinners brings the Pauline understanding of the co-redemption to heroic lengths.

In her unfailing commitment to follow Christ in the religious life beyond all human considerations, she told herself, "Either die, or conquer!" She is an aristocrat of love, charity, and supernatural willingness to undergo any hardship in order to be an instrument of God's mercy in this world.

Our Morning Offering will be filled with heroism, supernatural outlook, and fineness of feeling for Our Lord and the souls he puts in our path if we look to this devotion as guide and inspiration. Of course, we want to do more than simply follow an example, although that is a good thing to do too. Ultimately we must gain entrance through prayer and sacrifice to the Lord's heart as place of refuge.

As we have seen, our heart is meant to be a temple for the Holy Trinity, a cathedral lit by the fire of the Lord's charity, mercy, and infinitely holy presence. If this is to be so in our life, devotion to the Sacred Heart of Jesus shows us how. Only a heart in union with his heart could say with St. Paul, "It is no longer I who live, but Christ who lives in me" (Gal 2:20).

We on our part must not, in the words of Benedict XVI, deny God "the power to become small." It is indeed with the heart that we love. This center of fiery passion within a man or woman can move mountains with its fervor. Hearts become the field where seeds of grace grow into tall trees, with great, swaying branches that reach the throne of God with fruit that will last forever.

Our consecration to the Sacred Heart of Jesus is closely allied to the Immaculate Heart of Mary and the sacrament of the Eucharist.

To a world that chooses to see only what can be held, counted, or verified by its own standards, we must simply say that these mysteries are mysteries of love. Perhaps they suffer most who will not suffer for love. In any event, we make our Morning Offering ever mindful of the cost of sin and the price of our salvation to the very human heart of our divine Redeemer.

9. Holy Mass

In the Holy Mass what we do is adore: we fulfill lovingly the first duty of a creature to his Creator: You shall worship the Lord your God and Him only shall you serve. Not the cold, external adoration of a servant, but an intimate esteem and attachment that befits the tender love of a son.

—St. Josemaría Escrivá

How are we to live, each day, as children of God? We know by experience that we are full of defects, imperfections, sins imperfectly repented of, and even sins persisted in despite the misery they inevitably bring us. How are we to be worthy of the promises of Christ, as we say in the Angelus? How are we to live that union promised by the seeds of grace sown in our hearts at Baptism?

As Blessed Columba Marmion reminds us, our life should be a dying to self and sin—the plunge into Baptism being the death of our fallen nature's spurious rights—and a living in and for Christ our Redeemer, sent by the Father. But how are we to live with minds set on "things that are above" (Col 3:2) when we have such difficulty shaking off the petty things not of earth but of self? God in his infinite wisdom answers for us: the way to God *is* God in the holy sacrament of the Eucharist.

As the Israelites were fed by manna from the Lord while they wandered for forty years in the desert (Ex 16:35), so we are fed by a stronger food for a greater journey. We are told in St. John's gospel that those who eat this bread "will live forever" (Jn 6:58). To think about this possibility—everlasting life in the heart of God himself—for five minutes should change the way we live from this hour forward! For within this food is the giver of every gift, Christ himself. Whereas the other sacraments increase sanctifying grace in us, give it, or restore it, the Eucharist is itself the author of all graces. Our Lord has said it: "I am the bread of life" (Jn 6:48). This means we need to reflect with special reverence on the mystery of Holy Mass as we offer him each day as it comes from his hand.

In the shadow of his Cross, we learn how to pray, work, rejoice, suffer, serve, and persevere. So it should come as no surprise that Christ's sacrificial death should be the model of offering everything to God.

Each Mass reminds us that it is Christ who is the protagonist of our salvation, that while we must struggle with all our might to grow in charity and the virtues, we can do nothing good without him (Jn 15:5). Here is the perfection of our Morning Offering: not what we do for God but what he has done for us, particularly through the holy sacrifice of the altar.

The Mass is a sacrifice and a sacrament. Our Lord, at the Last Supper, left us this highest of gifts to remember what he had done for us on Calvary. So first, let us look at the sacramental nature of the Eucharist, since this "visible sign conferring invisible grace" is ordered toward Communion.[1] Here we must see this "remembrance" in the context of his unambiguous statement: "For my flesh is food indeed, and my blood is drink indeed" (Jn 6:55). As many Catholic theologians have noted, it is inconceivable that the apostles misunderstood Our Lord at this moment, he being the incarnate Word, knowing all things. If they were confused in this hour of immense significance, Our Lord would have known and clarified. He didn't clarify, of course, because he didn't need to. His apostles had come to believe that he was not only the long-foretold Messiah but also very God himself. Their First Communion was sacramental in the fullest sense: there were no barriers of misunderstanding as they were enfolded within the mystery of the Lord's salvific designs for the world.

The Fathers of the Church, who followed the apostles, teach the same doctrine of the Real Presence. Listen to St. Ignatius of Antioch, martyred in AD 110: "Come together in common, one and all without exception in charity . . . break one Bread which is the medicine of immortality and the antidote against death, enabling us to live forever in Jesus Christ."[2] St. Irenaeus of Lyons, in AD 180, said, "For just as the bread which comes from the earth, having received the invocation of God, is no longer ordinary bread, but the Eucharist . . . so our bodies, having received the Eucharist, are no longer corruptible, because they have the hope of the resurrection."[3] And St. Ambrose, in approximately AD 387, said, "Thus, every soul which receives the bread which comes down from heaven is a house of bread, the bread of Christ, being nourished and having its heart strengthened by the support of the heavenly bread which dwells within it."[4]

The promise of immortality refers to life everlasting, the resurrection of our flesh, in a new heaven and a new earth. But with the Eucharist, as Ambrose writes, we become, here, now, "a house of bread." This is a fascinating phrase, essentially translating Bethlehem, which in Hebrew means precisely that, house of bread.

Our Morning Offering deepens our interior life by drawing from the limitless graces of every offering of Holy Mass. Communion with Christ in the Eucharist is absolutely central to our life as Christians. Except for times when we forget to observe the fast, or find ourselves failing Our Lord in a serious matter, we should always approach the altar for Holy Communion with the awe, reverence, and adoration the Lord himself deserves and inspires.

There is another side to the depthless mystery of this great sacrament that is often overlooked today: this is the reality of the eucharistic *sacrifice* of the Mass as understood by sacred tradition.

In Abbot Vonier's *Key to the Doctrine of the Eucharist*, we read how "sacrifice is an act of religion, and therefore an act of justice, rendering to God what is His due . . . an act of fair and just dealing with God, wherein man, and even beast, is made to contribute to the recognition of God's sovereignty over all flesh."[5] This is why the sacrifices of the Old Testament are a "foreshadowing" of the sacrifice of the Cross: they were prescribed by Almighty God as a preparation for the New Covenant in Christ's blood for the life of the world.

A glance at our world today would tell us: sacrifice, joined to the perfect sacrifice of Christ, is the answer to the healing of souls, in this life and the next. There is no other hope frankly. Here is why it is essential that expression of our union with all the Masses throughout the world this day is at the center of our Morning Offering. This was the motivating force behind the Christocentric "New Evangelization" so often mentioned by St. John Paul II and continued by his successors: only the action of Christ himself can awaken the sleeping faith of those nations who have lost a sense of their Christian foundations, often set in place by the blood of martyrs over many centuries.

Almost a hundred years ago, as Alcuin Reid has pointed out, Dom Lambert Beauduin, in his *Liturgy: The Life of the Church*, expressed one of the central axioms of the liturgical movement of the twentieth century:

> For all alike, wise and ignorant, infants and adults, lay and religious, Christians of the first and Christians of the twentieth century, leaders of an active or of a contemplative life, for *all the faithful of the Church without exception,* the greatest possible active and frequent participation in . . . [the liturgy], according to the manner prescribed in

the liturgical canons, is the *normal and infallible path* to a solid piety that is sane, abundant, and truly Catholic, that makes them children of their holy mother the Church in the fullest sense of this ancient and Christian phrase.[6]

Holy Mass Is the Center of Everything

What our first parents lost at the dawn of our race by their own acts cannot be regained by our own efforts. John Paul II's apostolic exhortation *Reconciliatio et Paenitentia* makes a similar point, recognizing that these divisions in us wrought by sin go deep, requiring that our "reconciliation cannot be less profound than the division itself."[7] Yet our "active participation" in the liturgy must be properly understood. As Benedict XVI has reminded us, it must go beyond mere activism in the sanctuary and be rooted in an interior stillness and contemplative gaze open to grace.

According to the Council of Trent, the Mass "is a true sacrifice, properly so-called" and "in this Divine Sacrifice which is accomplished in the Mass there is contained and there is immolated in an unbloody manner the same Christ who, on the altar of the cross, offered Himself in a bloody manner. There is but one single Victim; and the same Christ who offered Himself upon the cross now offers Himself through the ministry of the priests; the manner of offering of Himself is the only difference."[8]

In the Mass, God directly acts through his ordained priest, however worthy or unworthy. By God's sovereign will during the consecration, the divine simplicity is at work: sacramental actions affect what they signify. At the words of Christ, on the lips of his priest, we are thus fed with nothing less than the bread of heaven. The food of the poor (we are all poor in God's eyes) now becomes at the Mass the means of offering anew the one sacrifice that opens heaven.

The priest, acting *in persona Christi*, becomes a living instrument of the true High Priest, Christ, who being both

God and man, can be a bridge, a *pontifex*, between fallen humanity and our Creator. We the laity, by virtue of our Baptism, truly assist in this awesome act. We can join in the sacrifice, offering our own sorrows and sufferings to those of Christ's. We place them with reverence on the paten of each Mass, and they are then drawn up into the one sacrifice of the Cross in a mysterious contemporaneity, to the awe of heaven and earth.

In all the long centuries of triumph, failure, and persecution, the Catholic Church has held to this doctrine with tenacity beyond all natural strength or explanation. Without doubt, the Eucharist is the most precious gift the Holy Trinity has given his Church. In the words of St. Maximilian Kolbe, "If angels could envy humanity, they would do so for only one reason: Holy Communion!"[9] Pope Benedict XVI has remarked that the Mass has been "disfigured" by innovations and abuses in the wake of the Second Vatican Council. Let us remind ourselves, with this wise pope, that the liturgy is not a "show" intended for our entertainment but the sacrifice of the Word-made-flesh to save us from eternal loss of his friendship.

The sacrificial nature of the Mass must be at the core of our eucharistic piety. As well, our reverent demeanor—how we dress, pray, speak, and act—must reflect this great mystery. When we offer our day in union with the countless Masses of each day, let us live St. Josemaría's advice: "God's love for his creatures is so boundless and our response to it should be so great that, when Holy Mass is being said, time ought to stand still."[10]

While there are many fine hymns and musical pieces expressing devotion to the Blessed Sacrament, perhaps none does so as admirably as "Adoro Te Devote," traditionally ascribed to St. Thomas Aquinas. In 1264, Pope Urban IV established the Feast of Corpus Christi. He asked Thomas to compose some prayers, hymns, and antiphons for the office of the Mass. Thomas complied, with the result being such lovely pieces as "Pange Lingua Gloriosi" and "O Sacrum Convivium."

"Adoro Te Devote" never made it into the Mass, but its manuscript survived and passed into St. Pius V's hands as he was compiling his Roman Missal of 1570. Pius V put the "Adoro Te Devote" among the prayers for preparation and thanksgiving for Holy Mass. From there, it spread among clergy and laity, receiving its most masterful translation into English by Jesuit father Gerard Manley Hopkins, one of the finest poets of Victorian England.

History, scripture, allegory, philosophy, devotion, and theology are compressed into an interwoven Latin text of both simplicity and subtlety. The first stanza sets the theme of the Lord's infinite transcendence and yet hidden, exquisite closeness in the sacrament. Here is the hymn, in Gerard Manley Hopkins's masterful translation:

Godhead here in hiding, whom I do adore,
Masked by these bare shadows, shape and nothing more,
See, Lord, at thy service low lies here a heart
Lost, all lost in wonder at the God thou art.

Seeing, touching, tasting are in thee deceived:
How says trusty hearing? that shall be believed;
What God's Son has told me, take for truth I do;
Truth himself speaks truly or there's nothing true.

On the cross thy godhead made no sign to men,
Here thy very manhood steals from human ken:
Both are my confession, both are my belief,
And I pray the prayer of the dying thief.

I am not like Thomas, wounds I cannot see,
But can plainly call thee Lord and God as he;
Let me to a deeper faith daily nearer move,
Daily make me harder hope and dearer love.

O thou our reminder of Christ crucified,
Living Bread, the life of us for whom he died,
Lend this life to me then: feed and feast my mind,
There be thou the sweetness man was meant to find.

Bring the tender tale true of the Pelican;
Bathe me, Jesu Lord, in what thy bosom ran—
Blood whereof a single drop has power to win
All the world forgiveness of its world of sin.

Jesu, whom I look at shrouded here below,
I beseech thee send me what I thirst for so,
Some day to gaze on thy face to face in light
And be blest for ever with thy glory's sight. Amen.[11]

These images are themselves a school of devotion. We should always give our eucharistic Lord ardent *adoratio*, worship, in a gaze of love. Indeed, gazing is how we adore. Our eye sees the "shape and nothing more" of the eucharistic "species"—the whiteness, the roundness of the bread—and our ear hears the words of Christ himself giving this gift to the apostles on the evening of Holy Thursday two thousand years ago. We see by divine faith our Eucharistic Lord.

This look of love gazes on Christ, the incarnate Word who is before us in the sacrament. Moreover, this looking, according to Josef Pieper, involves a foreshadowing of the quenching of the deepest thirsts inherent in our human condition, open to all who embrace the Faith. Pieper writes, "The ultimate fulfillment, the absolutely meaningful activity, the most perfect expression of being alive, the deepest satisfaction, and the fullest achievement of human existence must needs happen in the contemplating awareness of the world's ultimate and intrinsic foundations."[12] For this we were made.

We are called to adore as children of God. Augustine reminds us, "No one eats that flesh without first adoring it; we should sin were we not to adore it."[13] In this sacrament we see that Christ is the sum total of the Father's revelation to the world. While he walked the earth, one needed faith in Christ to see his divinity beyond the reality of his sacred humanity; now, in the sacramental life of his Church, even his *humanitas* is hidden in the appearances or the "accidents" of the bread and wine in the Eucharist.

The references to the Apostle Thomas and the good thief root our devotion in history. Thomas was able to see the wounds on the risen One and believe. The good thief could read with the eyes of faith the supernatural radiance behind the blood, sweat, and agony he shared with Christ on Calvary, and repent. In adoring our Lord, however, we now see only in the manner of a sacrament, a sign. Under this sign, we believe that Christ's body, blood, soul, and divinity are truly present. While the Lord's is truly there, his manner of presence is a substantial presence, with the accidents of the bread and wine held in place by the divine will. This act, the Council of Trent tells us, has no parallel in the entire world of nature.

"Adoro Te Devote" teaches us metaphysics set to the song of angels. We see the appearances of things with our senses; with our intellect, using the senses, we understand substance, what a thing is. The flavor of a medicine, for instance, can change while still being the same medicine. With the Eucharist, our senses can never see the reality of the Lord in the Sacred Host. This is precisely why supernatural faith opens the door to the sacramental gifts of the Lord. There is no other key.

For Aquinas, the object of our thirsting, of our faith, is always held in hope before us. The gift of both receiving and adoring Our Lord in the Eucharist gives witness to the life of our soul beginning now, sacramentally, in hidden form and, according to God's promise, will one day be so suffused by the light of his face that all desire will find its quenching, all yearnings their completeness, and all worthy hopes their fulfillment. This vision is an eternity of adoration.

Aquinas, writing in that sober tone that makes many of his insights easy to overlook, teaches us, "Faith is the foretaste of that knowledge that will make us happy."[14] The simplicity of this hymn expresses the depths and heights of prayer and a personal friendship with Christ, steeped in the scriptures and the Tradition of the Church. Quite a foretaste! Yet all this vast work of theology, noble as it is, remains merely preparatory: the souls of the just in heaven, says Thomas, see God in a direct, unmediated, endlessly delighting gaze.

As Benedict XVI put it, during the Mass, the "already" of heaven becomes one with the "not yet" of our earthly condition as pilgrims.[15] We should therefore savor the sweetness of the Lord in every Mass, knowing it is a promise and foretaste of what awaits us in hope. Let us with gratitude offer this day on the paten of every Mass offered over the entire world.

Let us too remember what St. John Chrysostom called "the liturgy after the liturgy" and, in another instance, the "sacrament of the brother and sister," along with his warning, "Do not therefore while adorning His house overlook your brother in distress, for he is more properly a temple than the other."[16] Far be it for us to join in a loving, tender, interior manner to the sacrifice of the altar and forget the needs and wounds of a broken world. As with the legendary pelican who fed its children from the blood of its own heart, so Christ has fed us with the blood of his most Sacred Heart. So should we do likewise, loving Our Lord and all souls from the depths of our heart with all we have.

How apt is that image of the pelican in evoking the self-giving of the saints of the Eucharist and the poor. Father Damien of Molokai, for instance, volunteered as a young religious to go to Hawaii to serve the lepers. St. Damien, canonized by Benedict XVI in 2009, was ordained shortly after arriving on the island of Oahu in 1864. After nine years of serving in parishes and helping the many ill due to poor health care, Damien volunteered to go to the island of

Molokai to care for 816 lepers, virtually abandoned by their government.

Upon arrival, he established a parish and built a perpetual adoration chapel where the lepers could bask in the loving presence of Christ. St. Damien himself drew strength from this gift as well, writing, "Without the constant presence of our Divine Master upon the altar in my poor chapels, I never could have persevered in casting my lot with the lepers of Molokai; the foreseen consequence of which begins now to appear on my skin, and is felt throughout the body. . . . I feel myself happy, well pleased, and resigned in the rather exceptional circumstances in which it has pleased Divine Providence to put me."[17]

St. Damien's ardent love for the Mass and adoration of the Eucharist became the "font and summit" of an apostolate that dressed wounds, healed souls, dug graves, and built homes. The island was transformed from within. Father Damien wrote his brother six months after arriving in Kalawao, the colony of outcasts: "I make myself a leper with the lepers to gain all to Jesus Christ."[18]

We should thank God for the priesthood every day, and pray for priests that they be as faithful as St. Damien! Pope Francis, in his homily for his first papal chrism Mass, draws an analogy from the priest's robes and anointing as symbols of service, done in the spirit of Christ:

> The sacred robes of the High Priest are rich in symbolism. One such symbol is that the names of the children of Israel were engraved on the onyx stones mounted on the shoulder-pieces of the ephod, the ancestor of our present-day chasuble: six on the stone of the right shoulder-piece and six on that of the left (cf. Ex 28:6–14). The names of the twelve tribes of Israel were also engraved on the breastplate (cf. Es 28:21). This means that the priest celebrates by carrying on his shoulders the people entrusted to his care and bearing their names written in his heart.[19]

With every Mass, the world is offered another chance at the renewal of all things by Christ's death and resurrection. Each day is a feast because each day we may partake of the bread of heaven, promise of eternal life.

As this image is a reminder for the priest to remember his flock, so too it is an incentive for the laity to bring their sorrows, their sufferings, their joys, and their hearts to the paten of each Mass. In this way, as coals burning with holy fire, fanning out in all directions, we will carry Christ's love to the highways and byways, bringing his light, joy, and peace into the world.

10. Thanksgiving

It is not unreasonable if the obligation of gratitude has no limit.

—St. Thomas Aquinas, *Summa Theologiae*, II.II.106.6

As we saw in an earlier chapter on offering our joys to God, we don't "offer up" only the hurtful things in our life. The latter is a crucially important act of piety, but it would fall terribly short if we kept all the goods of life to ourselves and only offered God our suffering. It would, in fact, gravely distort such an offering, root and branch.

God's sovereignty is over all that exists. He has a right to everything because everything comes from him—everything good that is. Hence we offer him everything, even the misuse of his gifts (our sins) in contrition, and our joys, which are his gift when they glow with truth. Once again, the act of offering thanksgiving back to the Lord preserves and extends the purity of our gratitude. For there can be a self-centered gratitude of the Pharisee: in his monologue that pretends to be prayer (Lk 18:11), the Pharisee thanks God that he is not like others whom he looks down upon for their obvious immorality. His thanksgiving is merely a mirror of his complacency born of pride, in which his self-love can gaze. This is not the kind of thanksgiving we want.

Instead, in the silence of prayer before the immensity of God's presence, we want to raise our hearts in thankfulness for all he has given us. We want our gratitude for God's favor to give wings to our hearts. We want to join our words to the heavenly liturgy so that our song of thanksgiving may soar beyond this world, giving us a foretaste of eternity, the morning that knows no evening. This is the thanksgiving that springs from a loving heart and makes our Morning Offering fresh each day.

Our Morning Offering should partake of the prayers of thanksgiving that the Lord has given his people, especially in the scriptures. We will close this chapter by noting a few of the more venerable ones. These prayers breathe a spirit of gratitude. They recognize that there are certain places, so to speak, that we cannot go without the right attitude or disposition.

For instance, reverence for the mystery of being and a sense of our own limitations are essential if we are to grow in the wisdom that comes from God. As Dietrich von Hildebrand wrote, "Reverence gives being the opportunity to unfold itself, to, as it were, speak to us."[1] Likewise, the broadening of the heart that comes from our thanksgiving increases our ability to see with the eyes of faith. In this way, we can avoid the distortions of selfishness and better realize how our merits are really God's crowning of his own gifts.

With the psalmist, we sing, "Enter his gates with thanksgiving, and his courts with praise! Give thanks to him, bless his name! For the Lord is good; his steadfast love endures for ever, and his faithfulness to all generations" (Ps 100:4–5). The key to the gates of the Lord's heart is thanksgiving. All that is lightsome, all that is freely given, and all that is faithful and pure in our hearts only dimly mirrors his freely given gifts of nature and grace. Our thanksgivings therefore should be joyful and lead us to rejoice with those who rejoice and console those in sorrow. In this way, our gratitude will partake of the Holy Spirit, "who has been given to us" (Rom 5:5).

For what favors are we grateful to the Lord? We give thanks for our existence, which was not our own doing. We are "wonderfully made" (Ps 139:14, MKJV), and our humanity is, even in its fallen state, a source of many blessings. Our ability to know—to become one with the object of our knowledge and to know something as it is—is directly related to our ability to love. What sublime gifts these are that distinguish us from the rest of the material creation!

We are thankful for the gift of our family, our parents, and their love, which cooperated with God's love in giving us life. Even with their flaws, their love shines bright. We are thankful for the gift of our Baptism, by which we were made children of God by adoption; for the priesthood, which brings countless sacramental graces into our living and our dying; and for the gift of Holy Matrimony, in which the good wine of Cana is celebrated in the love of a man and woman together for life, open to life, and the image of Christ's love for his bride, the Church.

We are thankful for the gift of forgiveness in the Sacrament of Confession—in which we rise from our sins by a loving embrace of the Father, bestowed by his Son, the eternal High Priest— and for the Sacrament of Anointing—which grants us holy strength in illness and in our final hour. We give thanks for the crowning of our Baptism in Confirmation, making us warriors for the peace of Christ that passes all understanding. We give unique thanksgiving for the sacrament of sacraments, the Holy Eucharist, which is the "font and summit" of a Christian's life, bread of angels, manna from heaven, and a foretaste of life eternal.

Of course, there is suffering, much of it unspeakably tragic. In a world bathed in the light of God, there are deep shafts of darkness. As we have seen, Christianity does not promise protection from suffering but offers a way to make our suffering redemptive by joining it to Christ's eternal offering on the Cross.

We can, even amid tears, thank him for allowing us to
join in a real way in the redemption of the world. St. Peter
reminds us that even in the crucible of suffering, a Christian
never loses hope in the Lord's ultimate promises: "Beloved,
do not be surprised at the fiery ordeal which comes upon
you to prove you, as though something strange were hap-
pening to you. But rejoice in so far as you share Christ's sufferings, that you may also rejoice and be glad when his glory
is revealed" (1 Pt 4:12–13).

Sharing in Christ's redemptive sufferings is no small
thing and can become a source of supernatural joy. How can
this be?

We must remember the light of Christian revelation
reveals that the foundation of the world is good. The world
we see before us, in all its intricate order and glorious beauty,
comes from the heart of the divine artist. After the six days
of creation, we read, "And God saw everything that he had
made, and behold, it was very good" (Gn 1:31). Later, the
book of Wisdom reads, "God did not make death, and he
does not delight in the death of the living. For he created
all things that they might exist" (Ws 1:13–14). The beauty
of creation is a trace, a reflection, as we have seen, of the
infinite beauty of the Creator. As Étienne Gilson reminds us,
"The work of creation is shattered, but the fragments remain
good, and, with the grace of God, they may be reconstituted
and restored."[2]

Poets express this elemental goodness in their works
when they give voice to the extraordinary beauty of ordinary
life. G. K. Chesterton, in his book on the medieval poet Geof-
frey Chaucer, captures perfectly this dazzling intuition of the
goodness of simply *being*:

> There is in the back of all our lives an abyss of light, more
> blinding and unfathomable than any abyss of darkness;
> and it is the abyss of actuality, of existence, of the fact that
> things truly are. . . . It is the fundamental fact of being, as

against not being. . . . That light of the positive is the business of the poets, because they see all things in the light
of it more than do other men. . . . Chaucer was a child of
light. . . . He was the immediate heir of something like
what Catholics call the Primitive Revelation; that glimpse
that was given of the world when God saw that it was
good. . . . Creation was the greatest of all Revolutions.[3]

Unlike the Gnostics over the centuries who tempted
many to follow their illusory spirituality, Catholicism does
not deem our suffering to be a "falling into flesh," as if we
were some spark struck from God that landed in the mud
and must endure the body until death reunites us with the
divine spirit. Of course, God is infinite, pure spirit, but *all* of
his creation is good, whether spiritual or material. We must
recognize and live "the primeval duty of praise." While evil
is undeniably a part of the world, it is not the first word and
certainly not the last.

The chief mystery of the Catholic Faith, after the Incarnation and Blessed Trinity, is the holy sacrifice of the Mass,
the Eucharist, which is the sacrificial *thanksgiving* offered by
God the Son, through the Holy Spirit, to the Father. All this is
given precisely so we may learn how to return in praise and
thanksgiving to God the gifts he has given us, extending St.
Augustine's advice for the Eucharist to our entire life: "We do
sin by not adoring."[4] Only then will our search for happiness
be on the right path to its final fulfillment.

Though God wills each person for his or her own sake
(so they might manifest his glory), all things exist not from
need, not by necessity, but from the abyss of divine goodness. When it comes to generosity, God's measure is simply
measureless. He is, in truth, the *giver* without peer. This is the
ultimate reason for our thanksgiving to God.

We should make many acts of thanksgiving, each hour
of our day, but particularly when we make our Morning
Offering. As Father Jacques Philippe wrote in his book on the

Holy Spirit, nothing wins more grace from God than when we thank him for every favor received. He cites a letter from St. Thérèse of Lisieux to her sister, explaining how this is: "What most draws graces from our dear Lord is gratitude, for it we thank him for a gift, he is touched and hastens to give us ten more, and if we thank him again with the same sincerity, what an incalculable multiplication of graces!"[5]

How can we best live this spirit of thanksgiving? First we must take stock of our spiritual life and make sure it has not fallen under the shadow of acedia, a gradually worsening condition that takes many manifestations, all of them enemies of the higher life of the soul.

Acedia is from Greek and literally means "not caring." It is a spiritual numbness, often masquerading as ceaseless activity. Monks for centuries have known it is a deadly affliction and not just for monks. Many of the world's problems are problems not of the intellect but of the will. St. Thomas Aquinas lists sloth ("acedia") and lust as the two major causes of despair. He even tell us that we can lose the taste for the things of God: "The fact that spiritual goods taste good to us no more, or seem to be goods of no great account, is chiefly due to our affections being infected with the love of bodily pleasures, among which, sexual pleasures hold the first place: for the love of those pleasures leads man to have a distaste for spiritual things, and not to hope for them as arduous goods. In this way despair is caused by lust."[6]

Acedia kills the spirit of thanksgiving at its root. Its deepest hope is not to be bothered by higher, more demanding things such as the moral life, the life of grace, and the calling of God. Avoiding acedia has nothing to do with a puritanical contempt for the pleasures of life. It is simply realism about the waywardness of our hearts as we seek to befriend Our Lord in a fallen world.

Second, with faith that can move mountains let us pray frequently those great prayers of thanksgiving, the *Te Deum* and the *Canticum Trium Puerum*, the "Canticle of the Three Children," which begins,

> Bless the Lord, all you works of the Lord;
> Praise and exalt him above all forever.
> Angels of the Lord, bless the Lord;
> You heavens, bless the Lord;
> All you waters above the heavens, bless the Lord.
> All you hosts of the Lord; bless the Lord.
> Sun and moon, bless the Lord;
> Stars of heaven, bless the Lord.
> Every shower and dew, bless the Lord;
> All you winds, bless the Lord.
> Fire and heat, bless the Lord;
> Cold and chill, bless the Lord.
> Dew and rain, bless the Lord;
> Frost and cold, bless the Lord.
> Ice and snow, bless the Lord.[7]

These hymns of praise, sung throughout the centuries, raise us to the heights of the Blessed Trinity, amidst the splendor of the eternal liturgy in heaven where countless choirs of angels and archangels rejoice in the glory of the Lord. In the canticle, drawn from the prophet Daniel, a thanksgiving literally arises from the crucible of suffering. The three children's praise of the Creator extends from the sun and moon and stars, to showers and dews, ice and snow, light and darkness, mountain and hills, seas and rivers, whales and fish of the sea, and birds of the air—in short, to the whole of creation, whose foundational goodness no evil can destroy.

Wendell Berry's poetry has a contemplative air and frequently reflects on what we have done with the riches of nature. His perspective is Christian, in a fairly inexact way, but one passage from his book *Leavings* captures well the sense of having a gift but forgetting the praise and gratitude due to all gifts and givers. He refers to this experience as the

"Heaven of knowing again," but from a Catholic perspective he is referencing purgatory, our final, painful school of thanksgiving where we are cleansed of our complacency:

> There is no marrying in Heaven, and I submit; even so,
> I would like to know my wife again, both of us young
> again, and I remembering always how I loved her
> when she was old. I would like to know
> my children again, all my family, all my dear ones,
> to see, to hear, to hold, more carefully
> than before, to study them lingeringly as one
> studies old verses, committing them to heart
> forever. I would like again to know my friends,
> my old companions, men and women, horses
> and dogs, in all the ages of our lives, here
> in this place that I have watched over all my life
> in all its moods and seasons, never enough.
> I will be leaving how many beauties overlooked?
> A painful Heaven this would be, for I would know
> by it how far I have fallen short. I have not
> paid enough attention, I have not been grateful
> enough. And yet this pain would be the measure
> of my love. In eternity's once and now, pain would
> place me surely in the Heaven of my earthly love.[8]

As sweet as it might be, the "heaven" of our "earthly love" is only a foretaste of the bliss of those who see God "as he is" (1 Jn 3:2). But how many times could each of us say with Berry that we have not been grateful enough for the blessings of our life? This is often the case in societies that suffer an excess of material comforts and lose sight of the supernatural purpose of mortification in order to keep keen their spiritual senses. True joy and lasting gratitude that well up from the heart are only found in souls who love. And love speaks, as it were, the language of offering. So in offering our day to God, we can linger, at least for a few moments, over the details of our daily life because each mundane detail when handed to the Lord will begin to glow with the fire from which all such gifts arise.

11. Reparation

Unless you repent you will all likewise perish.

—Luke 13:3

In devotion to the Sacred Heart of Jesus we are reminded of the necessity of reparation to God for our sins and the sins of the world, especially as they stem from ingratitude for divine favors we have received. By reparation we mean the part of penance that strives to join in the redemptive sufferings of Christ to make up for our sins and the sins of others. Our focus in this chapter will be on a simple question: *why* are we to join in the reparation Christ offers to the Father for the sins of the world?

Many over the years have the mistaken notion that Catholics believe we can *work* our way to heaven. One look at the teachings of the Church in this regard, however, should dispel such a notion. In *Miserentissimus Redemptor*, Pius XI clearly states, "The expiatory value of our acts depends solely upon the bloody sacrifice of Christ, a sacrifice which is renewed unceasingly in an unbloody manner on our altars."[1] This has been the constant teaching of the Church, based on scripture and Tradition and the lives of countless saints.

Our Lord's uncompromising demand in Luke 13:3 carries with it primarily the sense that we need to turn away from sin and return to a life of grace. But as St. Paul makes clear in his epistles (especially Col 1:24), and the Tradition of the Church underscores repeatedly, this "penance" or "meta-noia" has more than a single dimension. After giving primacy to the conversion from sin, penance traditionally includes fasting, almsgiving, and mortification. Reparation is that part or aspect of penance that seeks to make good, with grace, the moral and spiritual disorder of a past sin. Reparation often realizes these three traditional aspects of penance with the goal of making up for our past offenses and sins. As St. John Paul II reminds us, it must be intimately linked to conversion and reconciliation.[2]

Though God's forgiveness takes away the guilt of sin, the disorder in our souls and the dishonor done to God's infinite goodness still exists. This has less to do with images of God being "angered" over "insults" to his "majesty" than it does with the reality that sin is a profound wrong against the very nature of the ground of all that exists—the Lord himself.

In reforming the heart, the saints teach us that suffering is the most effective means. Even pagans saw this: Sophocles, in *Antigone*, refers to suffering as the primary path of purification that leads to wisdom. As Augustine writes, "Man is compelled to endure even when his sins are forgiven, although it was the first sin that caused his falling into such misery. For the penalty is more protracted than the fault, lest the faults should be accounted small."[3] We know that the humility, so to speak, of the sacraments can lull us into thinking they free us completely from hardship, suffering, penance, and reparation. Why they do *not* is related to the interiority of a person, however degraded by sin or ignorance.

When a human being transgresses a divine law, or a natural law, he or she makes a decision that misshapes that person's interior life. We become damaged by not living according to reality as transmitted to us by revelation or the light of reason. Likewise, when we follow the light of reason, that is, when we not only do but also actually embrace the divine will as expressed through the natural law, we flourish in ways specific to who we are as human beings.

Non-sentient (animal) nature, however variegated and wonderful, does not have the inner depths of a person. Aquinas saw this clearly: "Unconscious nature is more restricted and limited, while conscious nature has a greater breadth and reach. Aristotle had this in mind when he spoke of the soul as being somehow all things."[4] It shouldn't surprise us that repairing a cathedral is always more complicated than repairing a bird's nest.

The affections, the desires, the aspirations, the fears, and the countless habits which are ingrained in us so deeply that they nearly become identical with the self are all expressions of our interiority that can go astray, sometimes catastrophically. Paul Griffiths has shown with remarkable insight the complexity of a person's inner world in regard to his or her appetite for knowledge. Do we seek knowledge in a thirst for ownership, dominion, and mastery of the world that we come to know? Or do we see all knowledge as gift? Griffiths contemplates how the inner landscape of a person may become overrun with vices and whims so that the self becomes a wasteland, its ability to relate to the real all but shattered. He indirectly gives evidence of how penance and reparation are at times the only instruments by which grace may be able to reach such a soul:

> If, for example, you choose to indulge an appetite for dominating others so that you become habituated to the kinds of action that indulge such an appetite, you will be acting in a way unfitting for a human being, an image of God, and you will be responsible for doing so. You will be establishing ever more firmly your membership in the society of those the weight of whose desires is hurling them into the abyss.[5]

Griffiths goes on to explore how knowing may be safe-guarded or warped by a proper or improper "catechesis." He stresses that our self-damage, like our inherited damage (original sin), is utterly beyond our own ability to reform. Yet, with grace, the reformation of the individual soul is possible, "with God all things are possible" (Mt 19:26). The restoration of the human race is why God became incarnate in the first place.

How many great saints have themselves been turned by grace to a life of renewed piety and innocence, deepened by the debt of gratitude their own reclamation demands? In addition to the medicinal purposes of penance, then, comes reparation, born solely out of love. Here, love goes beyond the demands of justice, for the union of hearts in friendship and love always yearns for more than mere parity.

To a soul in love, nothing is more painful than to hurt the beloved. When the saints contemplate the infinite holiness of God, they of necessity see their own sins in an appallingly lucid light. In fact, when one loses one's sense of God, of his infinite transcendence and intimate presence in a soul in grace, sin becomes vague, shadowy, and theoretical. Or worse, one learns to focus on the faults of others, sometimes with a sharp eye and a grudging heart, until the rule mea-sured out to others takes no account of one's own sinfulness or the other's frailty. It is then that reparation and penance are desperately needed, for they keep the soul freshly aware of God's infinite mercy and our own need for that mercy.

This brings us back to the Sacred Heart of Our Lord. For when we sin, we offend the Trinity of persons in the inner-most life of God. As St. Margaret Mary Alacoque saw, the heart of our Redeemer is a furnace of self-giving love and an emblem of infinite mercy. We push that love away with the self-wounding of indifference and sin.

Reparation's role is to enter into this love—to, in a real sense, participate in its self-offering to the Father—by offering sacrifices in union with Christ's sacrifice on Calvary. Such souls become themselves incandescent with the fire of divine charity. No suffering is too much, even to the loss of all he or she holds dear in this world. St. Augustine puts it perfectly: "Give me a man that loves, and he feels what I say."[6]

Examples of saints whose hearts burned with the desire to make reparation come readily to mind: St. Paul, St. Matthew, St. Augustine, St. Benedict, St. Francis of Assisi, St. Ignatius of Loyola, St. Margaret Mary Alacoque, and St. Padre Pio, to name only a few. And who can forget the tears of the sinful woman who washed the Master's feet with costly perfumed nard? "Therefore I tell you, her sins, which are many, are forgiven, for she loved much; but he who is forgiven little, loves little" (Lk 7:47).

Here we touch on the deepest motive for reparation: love for the moral law, love for the truth at the expense of self, and love for goodness at the cost of everything one holds dear all find their perfection in the love of the Lord himself. Reparation is a mystery whose heights and depths are unfathomable, lost in the unsearchable riches of God's mercy (Eph 3:8).

As his humanity truly suffered and died, so did Christ's divine person experience the infinite sacrificial offering of the Cross, though as God he could not suffer any imperfection or loss of his divine plenitude. This is not, of course, to diminish what Christ suffered. He who lacks no perfection endured horrific pain and death simply to help us become his children by grace. Such generosity is limitlessly drawn from the well of divine goodness. This is part of that mysterious "kenosis," or emptying of the Lord, accepting for our redemption all the limitations, agonies, and finally, the pains of death. Pope Pius XI, in his encyclical on the mercy of God, draws our attention to the mystery of this self-emptying. God's personal incursion into history has implications for our prayers we offer to him today:

> Now if, because of our sins also which were as yet in the future, but were foreseen, the soul of Christ became

sorrowful unto death, it cannot be doubted that then, too, already he derived somewhat of solace from our reparation, which was likewise foreseen, when "there appeared to Him an angel from heaven" (Luke xxii, 43), in order that his Heart, oppressed with weariness and anguish, might find consolation. And so even now, in a wondrous yet true manner, we can and ought to console that Most Sacred Heart which is continually wounded by the sins of thankless men.[7]

The true meaning of reparation.

Christ's sacrifice was more than sufficient to enable the human race to attain the beatific vision in eternity.[8] God does not want us passively to accept his gifts, though their supernatural nature is entirely his. He wants us to join with him in the redemption of souls. We realize when a person has been robbed, or slandered, there must be reparation done before reconciliation is complete between God and the offender. Justice demands this. But once we grasp the invitation that God offers through reparation, we should hunger for the fullness of justice that is found in the perfection of all the virtues: charity. And what would charity not suffer for the good of the beloved?

We can scarcely imagine the clarity of light and strength brought to Our Lord by that angel from heaven. St. Luke is the only evangelist to make a reference to the event (Lk 22:43). His visit emphasizes Our Lord's humanity as it was wounded by the weight of our sins. As we know, Gethsemane means "olive press" for its trees that yield healing oil when their fruit is crushed. And crushed he was, "bruised for our sins."

As Abbot Vonier puts it, echoing St. Thomas, "In one way or another, every sacrament is the fire of Christ's love when he was dying on the Cross."[9] While not refusing his Father's will in the least, Christ suffered from his natural flinching from anticipated pain and his vision of the nearly endless spectacle of human malice, greed, anger, envy, pride, and lust bringing death to souls over the centuries preceding his passion and following it.

The chalice that Christ had to drink from was filled with the gall of his coming betrayal, the foulness of false accusations, and the myriad impurities of a world in love with gifts twisted and betrayed. All these spiritual and psychological agonies made his body break into a sweat of blood. The darkness of Gethsemane must have accentuated the loneliness of his suffering. Gone were the nights of relaxing in the coolness of the olive trees with his apostles, their chanted psalms intoning the greatness of God's law and promises. Now those apostles were overcome with sleep, and the flicker of torchlight and the clanking armor of temple guards would soon begin the "hour" of "the power of darkness" (Lk 22:53). Christ grasped with trembling hand the weight of the chalice as he sought the strength of will to bring it to his lips and drink the sorrows of the world.

When we offer reparation for our sins and for sins of the world, we share in this angel's mission of comforting Christ.

Though now he is in glory in heaven, to suffer no more, the witness of his Passion still stands before the Father. The hours of his suffering were suffered according to his divine person, and so he saw all the times, hours, and minutes of history, down to their smallest detail. As the angel sent by the Father illuminated the darkness of the garden, what visions and wordless encouragement must have streamed forth from that heavenly intellect into the suffering heart of Christ?

Our Lord must have seen then the Church, the ark of salvation, sailing through the waters of history, pitching and rolling in times of persecution yet regaining its balance in the stormiest seas. He must have seen his apostles in their newfound strength brought on by the fires of Pentecost, bravely enduring every torment the Roman Empire could hurl at them, and paving the way for countless converts, and even entire lands, to enter the Church by their testimony of martyrdom. Christ must have seen the supernatural charity with which so many bishops, priests, deacons, and holy men and women have given their lives for the truth of his Gospel even while forgiving their persecutors with their dying breaths. He must have seen the tens of thousands of religious saving an entire legacy of a civilization as the Roman cities eroded in the winds of neglect and ruin brought by hungry tribes from the north, who would, in their turn, embrace the Faith that is always new.

Our Lord must have seen, in that brilliantly illuminated moment, lit by the hand of his Father's angel, the purity, devotion, and humility of so many hundreds of millions of Christians who have offered their sufferings in reparation for the sins of so many blinded by the false gods and demons that haunt this world. His bride, the Church, declared dead, was now rising before the astonished eyes of unbelievers, "terrible as an army with banners." His bride still holds out hope for all who believe that the same love which made the universe has broken the bonds of death that mere creatures, however gifted, can never escape on their own.

So too, Christ must have seen how that impetuous fisherman named Peter, the rock, would form a line of men— some humble and holy, some brilliant, and some giving heed to no world but this one (but for all that a link in a magnificent line)—that would extend out to the last syllable of recorded time, calling us to God, to charity, and to join the ranks of endless pilgrims who see life as a gift, but also as a prelude that bears within it seeds of future glory.

Our Lord must have seen all this and more in his hour of agony in the garden. What greater motive for reparation could there be? What greater hope could we have than eternal life won for us by the blood of Christ?

Our Morning Offering should be filled with hope, knowing that with the Virgin Mary, our Mother, in union with the sacrifice of the Mass over the entire world, we can plead for souls, offering sacrifices and prayers of reparation for our sins and the sins of the whole world.

Since we are all prodigal children of the Father, in one way or another, in order to find a further motive for reparation, we might imagine what the prodigal son in the gospel parable was doing the next morning, after having been forgiven and fêted with his father's blessings. My bet is that the fine robe he was given would have been carefully put away, and he would be out early in the fields, loins girded, and eager to help his father in every way possible.

12. *A*postolate

If leaven is not used for fermenting, it rots.

—St. Josemaría Escrivá

Today's reigning wisdom would have us avoid at all costs upsetting our neighbors by explaining a view of life or morality that contradicts theirs. This isn't an understandable forgoing of rough manners, disrespect, or manipulation; everyone should avoid these as they conflict with charity, the highest good. What the postmodern ethic calls for is something truly pernicious: we are forbidden, on pain of ostracism, from speaking what we believe is the truth when others in the room think differently.

Mahatma Gandhi once called proselytism "the deadliest poison that ever sapped the fountain of truth."[1] Unfortunately, this statement, founded on the metaphysics of Eastern religions and coupled with the widespread skepticism of the West, has helped bring us to the point of where most see truth as the enemy of democracy and pluralism. The liberating nature of truth has been made to appear its exact opposite: truth now burdens, isolates, and even enchains. It is now thought that tolerance, not truth, will set us free. Living this way, however, we will only surrender ourselves to a conspiracy of silence that is opposed to living an authentically human life which must always be shaped by the truth.

Truth is inescapable. It is the very element in which we live and move, without which we would have as much chance of living as we would of surviving in the vacuum of space. Even the pragmatic Marxists claimed to have grabbed hold of the way things really are. It's unavoidable.

For instance, "'There is no truth,' said one. The other said: 'But you are yourself assuming that it is a truth that there is no truth.'" In this brief dialogue, Max Picard shows us that "through the logic that is in language from the beginning" language itself makes truth manifest.[2] To deny language's link with truth is logically to forgo any speech at all. That we keep on speaking shows less the impotence of logic than the inescapable desire we have for knowing, even if we think the thing we know is ultimately noise from the nameless void. Yet our desire is not in vain, as we were made by the Word of God, and when we utter truths we do so in his light that he has given us by virtue of our humanity (Ps 36:9).

In our Morning Offering, we want to remember the intentions of our friends and relatives. This means doing apostolate with them, which according to St. Josemaría Escrivá, should be born of "confidence and friendship."[3] Where there is genuine friendship and confidence based on trust, there can never be any reason to act in any way that would bring to mind the negative associations that have nearly ruined the word *proselytize*. Moreover, because Christianity sees the human person as made in the image and likeness of God, any manipulation or material incentive to embrace the truth of Christ betrays the spirit of the Gospel.

The Second Vatican Council, in perhaps one of its most central but as yet underappreciated teachings, tells us that the laity practice their "apostolate in fact by their activity directed to the evangelization and sanctification of men and the perfecting of the temporal order through the spirit of the Gospel. Since the laity live in the midst of the world and its concerns, they are called by God to exercise their apostolate in the world like leaven, with the ardor of the spirit of Christ."[4]

This is the vocation of the everyday Christian living close to Christ, in the midst of the world.

We are to be like "leaven" (Mt 13:33), lifting all things to God by word and example, or like "salt" (Mt 5:13), overcoming evil with goodness, preserving the Word of God in our hearts and bringing it to everyone we meet, especially those who are poor, forgotten, or living without hope. By the strength of our Christian witness, we must renew "the temporal order," which really means renewing the day that lies before us. This is one of the aims of our Morning Offering: to renew the world from within by offering our day and ourselves to God.

Doing apostolate means being an apostle of Jesus Christ. The word *apostle* comes from a Greek word, conveying a sense of being sent, of being commissioned, deputized, authorized, and in fact, ordered to go out to others, to reach them and speak to them of the *evangelium*, the good news of Christ. This sending forth is integrally related to Christianity's reality as revelation. As Pope Benedict XVI put it in his first encyclical, becoming a Christian is "not the result of an ethical choice or a lofty idea, but the encounter with an event, a person, which gives life a new horizon and a decisive direction."[5]

The Old Testament often depicts the spiritual life in images of water flowing from a fountain. In the Middle East, of course, this would be a natural reference to a necessity of life amid the seemingly unending desert. But this image is also a reminder of the depths of the soul thirsting for God and the blessed ones that have found him: "The words of a man's mouth are deep waters; the fountain of wisdom is a gushing stream" (Prv 18:4). The graces of God know neither end nor limit. He is infinitely generous to those who seek him, for the soul that lives by him is "like a tree planted by streams of water, that yields its fruit in its season, and its leaf does not wither" (Ps 1:3).

These images of thirst and its fulfillment find their culmination in Christ: "On the last day of the feast, the great

day, Jesus stood up and proclaimed, 'If any one thirst, let
him come to me and drink. He who believes in me, as the
scripture has said, "Out of his heart shall flow rivers of living
water"'" (Jn 7:37–38). Christ is the "rock" out of which all
healing and life-giving graces flow (1 Cor 10:4). He is also the
Lord of the universe, through whom all things were made,
and in the end, all things will give witness to his glory. St.
John's vision of the heavenly liturgy puts Christ at the center,
described in images that are clearly tied to the prophecy of
his coming: "And he said to me, 'It is done! I am the Alpha
and the Omega, the beginning and the end. To the thirsty I
will give water without price from the fountain of the water
of life'" (Rv 21:6).

God is the harvester of souls; we are only his servants.
But if we are to be apostles of Christ, we must train ourselves to be ready instruments of God's love. We should drink
deeply of God's truth if we want to bring his good news to
a world thirsting for him. We should live, then, these four
basic realities if we want to help people come closer to God:

Reality 1:
The Need to Cultivate the Interior Life

This is absolutely first in the life of an apostle. We will be
useless to Our Lord if we are not striving to become saints.
We must banish from our lives and thoughts what Dom
Jean-Baptiste Chautard referred to as "the heresy of good
works."[6] Only a life in union with the heart of God will bring
others to God. This means an intense participation in the liturgical life of the Church, with Holy Mass as the "source and
summit" of all we are and all we do. Our interior life—loving
conversation with the Lord—must be habitual and fed with
sacrament, prayer, and sacrifice. The works we do should be
an overflow of this divine life within us. The spirit of divine
filiation should be the bedrock of our life.

We are, after all, by the grace of Baptism, children of God. For most people, some spiritual direction with a priest of sound doctrine is a necessity if we are to live as such. As well, yearly retreats and, if possible, monthly time away from work for a morning or evening will help immensely in this essential task, or rather, this manner of living as a child of God. We must go out into the deep, "duc in altum" to bring as many fish into the bark of Peter as possible (Lk 5:4). We must remember that this command of Christ's also refers to the depths of the spiritual life, born of sacramental grace and living in the presence of God. On our own we are coals rapidly losing light and heat. "Apart from me you can do nothing" (Jn 15:5).

Reality 2:
The Need to Attend to Love and the Moral Life

Because love is the highest virtue, to be authentic, love must be ordered first to God and then, guided by his light and truth, strive for human and supernatural virtues. We are not stoics, but we must have immense fortitude. We are not angels, so we must embrace purity of heart, mind, and body. Although we must not fall into legalism, we must practice justice down to the last detail, giving what we owe, and more, for souls.

We must always remember how mercy perfects justice. Above all, we must make all our decisions inside, so to speak, the virtue of prudence—not a calculating, worldly prudence but true prudence, the mother of the virtues, which takes as its measure *reality*. Dom Chautard saw rightly: "My interior life will be no better than my custody of heart."[7] With these human virtues, we must live, above all, the supernatural virtues of faith, hope, and love. These are infused into our souls with sanctifying grace. They are principles of being and acting, according to the wisdom of the saints, who know the heart of God.

Reality 3:
We Must Make a Priority of Family Life

This is a consequence of living one's vocation to holiness based on the Sacrament of Baptism yet in a way specific to the individual. There are two ways of living this out: either in the Sacrament of Matrimony or in the single life, which could include a life of apostolic celibacy. In either case, one must live family life, as the father or mother of a family, or in friendship with one's own family, one's parents, siblings, and wider relatives, including of course friends.

Marriage should be considered, as it truly is, a path to sanctity. Indeed, the seedbed of religious and priestly vocations, as well as vocations to celibacy in the middle of the world, is the family. But one might as truly say that the family is the seedbed of sanity. We ignore the family at our own peril. As G. K. Chesterton put it, "This triangle of truisms, of father, mother and child, cannot be destroyed; it can only destroy those civilizations which disregard it."[8]

Reality 4:
We Must Balance Home and Work

Whether we work on a vineyard in the sight of the Andes or in an office in Manhattan, or drive a truck across the highways of Canada, we usually will find ourselves immersed in adult life in the world of work. Some cultures show a better balance between work and family than others, while many societies, particularly in the United States, for instance, tend toward an imbalance, giving too much time and attention to work while other crucial aspects of life are left to fend for themselves. This has caused great harm to marriages and families. To offer our work to the Lord, as we said in chapter 4, it must not be disordered; it must not be, in a sense, stolen from our family, or from God himself, and then offered to him. This would be an unworthy offering.

The quality, balance, and devotion with which we work will be a strong incentive for our friends to listen to what we have to say about God. As well, to give God time every day for prayer is, of course, to return his own gift, but it is also a silent witness to the primacy of *being* over action, to the principle that he is the vine, and we are the branches. Our work itself can then become prayer because it overflows from our hearts that seek to live every moment immersed in God.

The Morning Offering of Thérèse, the Little Flower

Our Morning Offering attains infinite value because of the One to whom it is offered. Prayer becomes a spiritual lever, so to speak, with which we can move mountains or, even more amazingly, the hearts of our relatives and friends (in God's good time), and of countless souls too, who by God's grace, we will only meet in heaven. St. Thérèse of Lisieux saw this reality with all her soul, and it made her overflow with supernatural charity, with acts of faith and hope too large for this world. In her small corner of France, during her relatively short twenty-four years of life, St. Thérèse became the model for missionaries, apostles, theologians, parents, and those doing battle with hostile forces that will not recognize God's dominion over all, which is a dominion of love.

Let us make our Morning Offering with the same confidence and faith in God as Thérèse, the Little Flower, did in her earthly life. Let's make our Morning Offering with all the ardor of a soldier of Christ who wields the sword of truth: "To be Thy spouse, O my Jesus, to be a daughter of Carmel, and by my union with Thee to be the mother of souls, should not all this content me? Yet other vocations make themselves felt, and I would wield the sword, I would be a Priest, an Apostle, a Martyr, a Doctor of the Church, I would fain accomplish the most heroic deeds—the spirit of the Crusader burns within me, and I would gladly die on the battlefield in defense of the Church."[9]

St. John Paul II declared St. Thérèse a doctor of the universal Church on October 19, 1997.

13. The Holy Father

The Pope, who comes of Revelation, has no jurisdiction over nature.

—Blessed John Henry Newman

Our Lord's so-called High Priestly Prayer, in the seventeenth chapter of the Gospel of St. John, is rich with truths about God and his Church. It is no surprise that Christ's prayer for the unity of his disciples has immense implications for the life of a believer and for the life of the world. The unity of which he speaks is not the unity of a lifeless thing. It is not the conformity of inert beings to physical laws. It is certainly not the unity that comes from fear, a counterfeit unity in which the desire to flee is overridden by a fear of the consequences of doing so.

The unity of which Christ speaks is both a partaking of his unity with his Father and also, somewhat mysteriously, a visible sign that is evidence of his presence in his Church to the end of time: "I do not pray for these only, but also for those who believe in me through their word, that they may all be one; even as thou, Father, art in me, and I in thee, that they also may be in us, so that the world may believe that thou hast sent me" (Jn 17:20–21). This unity is pledge and witness, and its earthly focal point is Peter and his successors.

The testimony of scripture concerning St. Peter's primacy among the first apostles is abundant and clear. The papacy was prefigured in many ways in Isaiah 22:15–24 in the office of the steward of the royal household of King Hezekiah. In the New Testament, in the Acts of the Apostles and in the Council of Jerusalem, Peter is decisively leader of the Church. His preeminence is implicit in the several listings of the apostles in which his name comes first. These details, of marginal weight perhaps in themselves, are like small brush strokes that fill in the portrait of Peter drawn in Matthew 16. To explain away the gift of the keys by linguistic ingenuity is to throw the whole pattern of Christ's foundational actions as recorded in scripture into incoherence. When there is no single, visible source of unity, revelation—divine speech to humanity—becomes impossible.

The Fathers of the Church frequently cite Peter's primacy. In the year AD 110, for instance, in St. Ignatius's "Letter to the Romans," we find this greeting: "Ignatius . . . to the church that is in charge of affairs in Roman quarters. You are a credit to God: you deserve your renown and are to be congratulated. You deserve praise and success and are privileged to be without blemish. Yes, you rank first in love, being true to Christ's law and stamped with the Father's name."[1]

In AD 190, only several generations after the death of St. John, we hear St. Clement of Alexandria refer to the first bishop of Rome in the following terms: "The blessed Peter, the chosen, the pre-eminent, the first among the disciples, for whom alone with himself the Savior paid the tribute."[2] Likewise, there is the clear voice of Optatus, the fourth-century bishop from Numidia who fought with Augustine against the Donatists, schismatics who thought personal sin could corrupt the efficacy of the sacraments: "You cannot deny that you are aware that in the city of Rome the episcopal chair was given first to Peter; the chair in which Peter sat, the same who was head—that is why he is also called Cephas—of all the apostles; the one chair in which unity is maintained by all."[3]

These early testimonies of the primacy of the bishop of Rome are moving in their devotion to the unity of the Church, a gift of God and sign of its divine institution. Reading them, we can well see why Blessed John Henry Newman would write, centuries later, "To be deep in history is to cease to be a Protestant."[4]

When we conclude our Morning Offering with a reference to the intentions of the pope, we are praying for something that partakes of a belief in God's dramatic incursion into human history. Though many today fail to understand this devotion to the bishop of Rome, it is at the heart of the Catholic Faith. As we said, Christianity itself stands or falls on this visible sign of unity.

For if God did truly become a man on a specific day in a specific year, in a town in a definite part of the world, born to a woman married and yet a virgin, and over skies of a single night like no other in human history, then it only follows that this God-made-man would give us a way to take hold of his message with all the certainty due to such a message and such an event. Indeed, to diminish or dismiss the Petrine office is necessarily to deny the reality of the Incarnation. If God were to speak with humanity, surely he would find a way to keep the integrity of his message intact for the generations that follow that initial gift. An incoherent answer is as good as no answer at all.

He has left us an answer, of course, and a means to keeping it in its fullness to the end of time: "When the Spirit of truth comes, he will guide you into all the truth; for he will not speak on his own authority, but whatever he hears he will speak, and he will declare to you the things that are to come" (Jn 16:13). Our Lord does this by the scandal of having instituted a perpetual office beyond the capacity—morally and spiritually—of any mortal. "Put not your trust in princes" (Ps 146:3) is in fact at the root of this article of Faith, for in trusting the Holy Father, the bishop of Rome, we trust not the man per se but the office entrusted to him by Almighty God.

This *scandal* is the perennial temptation of fallen humanity: to think that the God of all being is incapable of specific action, of individual choice, of acting here and now, in this moment, and keeping the promise of that moment for all time. Yet, in truth, we wrongly restrict God when we disallow him such freedom.

George Weigel, in his *Letters to a Young Catholic*, has written on this aspect of the papacy in his chapter on the burial chambers below the Basilica of St. Peter's in Rome. In 1939, on the eve of the Second World War, Pius XII ordered that the floor of the basilica be lowered to make room for the tomb of his deceased predecessor, Pius XI. Excavators uncovered a large necropolis of pagan and early Christian graves dug deep into the soil of Vatican Hill. They also uncovered walls from Constantine's basilica built in the fourth century, which form the foundation of the massive present-day basilica built in the sixteenth century.

At this burial site, called the *scavi* (from the Italian for excavation), workers discovered the remains of a man who scientists have determined was of solid build and in his mid-sixties. Graffiti in ancient Greek indicates, "Peter is." The bones were wrapped in silk threads dyed Tyrian purple, a sign of royal dignity in the ancient world. One doesn't have to be a Catholic to conclude that these bones belong to the first bishop of Rome.

At street level, the grave of the first pope is directly below the basilica's main altar and gorgeous baldacchino, designed by Bernini and completed in 1633. Weigel also notes the 350-ton Egyptian monolith now in St. Peter's square, brought to Rome by Caligula and used in Nero's so-called circus where many Christians, including St. Peter, met their martyrdom. Pope Sixtus V moved the monolith to its present location in 1586.

In all likelihood, this monolith, with its straight, unyielding lines and massive weight immovable except for teams of slaves and draft animals pulling ropes for months, was the last thing St. Peter saw before he died. What was this prince of the apostles thinking during his final hour? Perhaps he was wondering how the hearts of those putting him to death were as immoveable as that granite obelisk, except for grace. We will never know this side of eternity. The empire that crucified him long ago has vanished, it remains turned over to the worship of Christ, or the gaze of tourists.

Weigel writes, "The scavi and the obelisk confront us with the historical tangibility, the sheer grittiness, of Catholicism. Catholicism does not rest on pious myth, a story that floats away from us the more we try to touch it. Here, in the *scavi*, we're in touch with the apostolic foundations of the Catholic Church. And those foundations are not in our minds. They exist, quite literally, in reality."[5]

This is a fine, sturdy reminder of the uniqueness of Catholicism and its inherent realism. These apostolic foundations also remind us that Catholicism is not, at its heart, man's search for God but God's search for humanity in the Incarnation. In his infinite majesty, God does not disdain the manger or the Cross. Given human waywardness, it is perhaps an even greater humbling of God to submit to the staggering paradox of allowing down through the centuries a mere man, a single mortal, to bind and loose on earth what will be honored in heaven.

Unfortunately, many think of the pope as a ruler who can do anything he wants, an autocrat with a blank check issued by the Fathers of Vatican Council I and endorsed by God. This is a seriously deficient understanding of what the office of the bishop of Rome really is, and therefore a disservice to God and his Church. The calls for the new pope, before the election of Francis in 2013, to allow women to become priests, to approve of homosexual marriage, or some other such so-called liberalizing of the Catholic Church are founded on precisely such a misunderstanding.

Blessed John Henry Newman was apprehensive about the results of Vatican I before they were made public. He was hoping that the Ultramontantists—those who wanted nearly unlimited papal authority—would not overreach and make the council declare something beyond what Tradition could countenance. Newman had no doubts that the pope partook of the infallibility Christ promised to his Church, but he thought such a declaration in 1870 would be untimely. When Newman finally received word of the definition of infallibility declared by the council, he was pleased with its moderation.[6] As we make our Morning Offering, it will surely be helpful to review briefly that same definition and see why it is such a blessing to the Church and the world.

Session 4, chapter 4, of the *First Dogmatic Constitution on the Church of Christ* reads like a drumroll of preceding councils asserting the same supernatural prerogative for the bishop of Rome. Citing the fourth Council of Constantinople (869–870), the second Council of Lyons (1272), the Council of Florence (1431), and all "venerable fathers" and "all the holy orthodox doctors," the First Vatican Council affirmed solemnly,

> We teach and define that it is a dogma divinely revealed: that the Roman Pontiff, when he speaks *ex cathedra*, that is, when, in discharge of the office as pastor and teacher of all Christians, by virtue of his supreme Apostolic authority, he defines a doctrine regarding faith and morals to be held by the universal Church, is, by the divine assistance promised to him in Blessed Peter, possessed of that infallibility with which the divine Redeemer willed that His Church should be endowed.[7]

Newman noted that the word "assistance" was significant, for the pope is not an oracle, not inspired by the Holy Spirit in the manner of the first apostles, nor is he exempt from the demands of study and prayer while consulting, indeed, deeply pondering, the teaching of the Church as manifested in scripture and tradition. Newman leaves no doubt that the Petrine Office is the servant of revelation, not its master: "As a definition of faith must be drawn from the

Apostolic *depositum* of doctrine, in order that it may be considered an exercise of infallibility, whether in the Pope or a Council, so too a precept of morals, if it is to be accepted as from an infallible voice, must be drawn from the Moral law, that primary revelation to us from God."[8]

Vatican II maintained this doctrine of papal infallibility while underscoring the role of the college of bishops around the world in union with the Holy Father. In *Lumen Gentium*, the Pastoral Constitution on the Church, we are reminded that the Lord "in order that the episcopate itself might be one and undivided . . . placed Blessed Peter over the other apostles, and instituted in him a permanent and visible source and foundation of unity of faith and communion."[9]

In this way, the Church is telling us what the Petrine Office offers to us: "a permanent and visible source and foundation" so that from the deposit of faith given to the apostles and then handed on to their successors, we may drink from the springs of living water a faith undefiled and true. A note attached at the end of this document makes clear that the college of bishops is not founded on a democratic principle but is from revelation itself.

Thus the marks of the Church—its unity, holiness, catholicity, and apostolicity—are signs observable to all and yet nevertheless partake of the mystery of God. Though the sins of its members may at times almost wholly distort its outward visage, the Church remains not only rooted in history but also preeminently rooted in the mystery of the God who founded it in a moment of time to last until the end of time. As Cardinal Charles Journet writes, its "apostolic character . . . will be no less mysterious than the Church herself. We believe in apostolicity as we believe in the Church: *Credo . . . apostolicam Ecclesiam*."[10]

We should rejoice at the clarity of teaching provided us by our Catholic Faith and the institution of the papacy in particular. Yes, there have been spectacularly bad men on the chair of Peter. Yet nearly a third of the 265 successors of St. Peter have been declared saints. Certainly, in modern times, we have had a long line of either highly decent, even saintly, men as the bishop of Rome and pastor of the universal Church. Yet, as Chesterton put it in *Heretics*, the Church has survived not because it is founded "by strong men and upon strong men" but because it has been founded by Almighty God and his promises do not fail.[11] Hence the wounds of the Church, though more painful when self-inflicted, only show forth her glorious, unearthly origin even amid the worst, most dreadfully human failures.

While the Church is clearly, from its institution by Christ the Lord, hierarchical (as restated at Vatican II, in *Lumen Gentium*, chapter 3), and the Holy Father is the supreme pontiff of the universal Church, there is another profile, so to speak, of the Church that is not only consonant with its founding but also actually prior to the Petrine ministry. This profile is found in the person of a simple girl who from the moment of her conception in her mother's womb was destined to be the Mother of God and the Queen of Heaven and Earth.

On December 22, 1987, Pope John Paul II, in his address to the Roman curia, reminded his cardinals that, in words that are now part of the *Catechism of the Catholic Church*, "The Marian dimension of the Church is antecedent to that of the Petrine, without being in any way divided from it or being less complementary. The Immaculate Mary precedes all others, including obviously Peter himself and the Apostles" (*CCC*, 773). This statement is rich with implication but essentially puts the offices of the Church in their proper perspective—that is, by seeing them in their service to the truth.

The Holy Father for whom we pray each day is there to preserve the gift of Christ's revelation so we might feast on the truth that will bring us to God. Seeing the pope as some spiritual CEO, with a board that is only distinguished by their proclivity for red and black, is to miss entirely the significance and purpose of why we have a pope in the first place.

Though the abuses of authority in the Church over the centuries weigh on the heart of each believer, the light reflected in the face of the Virgin Mary, the Mother of the Church, is the light of her divine Son. She is, in fact, *spes nostra*, our hope, precisely because of this joyful truth. The Mother of Sorrows is also the Queen of Apostles because she knows that the Cross leads to the morning of the resurrection. In this ever-fresh light of eternity, she now sees her Son in the heart of the eternal and perfect self-giving of the Blessed Trinity.

As Pope Benedict XVI put it, summing up Mary's relation to the Church as reiterated by Vatican II, "Mary is so interwoven in the great mystery of the Church that she and the Church are inseparable, just as she and Christ are inseparable. Mary mirrors the Church, anticipates the Church in her person, and in all the turbulence that affects the suffering, struggling Church she always remains the Star of salvation. In her lies the true center in which we trust, even if its peripheries very often weigh on our soul."[12]

For this reason, when we put our prayers for the Holy Father on the paten of the Mass each morning, let us remember his intentions and throughout the day remember him with renewed love and affection. Let us joyfully remember that the infallibility of the Church and the office of Peter are, ultimately, Marian mysteries. The Church's indefectible holiness—through her sacraments and teaching—partakes of the Virgin Mary's holiness, Ark of Salvation, and Refuge of Sinners.

As such, these mysteries serve that greater unity that Christ enjoys with his Father in eternity. Our Lady is before them, body and soul; she is the image of the Bride of Christ, the Church, born now in the heart of each of the faithful as we make our pilgrimage to our true homeland beyond death, where the light of faith will flower into the light of glory that will never fade.

There are more spiritual riches, more theology, and more
piety than we might at first think in that simple aspiration
"omnes cum Petro ad Jesum per Mariam"—all with Peter to Jesus
through Mary.

14. *A*men

Though in intention our offering lasts all day, with this simple word we bring our prayer of the Morning Offering to
a close. We are used to saying "amen" as a conclusion to
vocal prayers said either in private or with others and in the
prayers spoken or sung in the liturgy of the Church. We'll
let scripture scholars debate the word's origins and layers of
meaning, but for our reflections on offering our day to the
Lord, a couple of ideas are especially relevant.

The first one comes from Pope Benedict XVI's *Introduction to Christianity*, originally written as a series of lectures
in the summer term of 1967 at the University of Tubingen.
Benedict's reflections on the Faith as the very ground of the
universe is a good place for us to conclude our reflections on
the Morning Offering, whose height and depth are no less
than the heart of the living God as revealed in Jesus Christ.

In St. Matthew's gospel, Our Lord says "amen" twen-
ty-eight times. St. John gives us twenty-six occasions in which
Jesus uses a double form of the word to introduce a statement,
invariably one of special importance. In the Old Testament
the double usage is unheard of, while the single amen is most
commonly found punctuating a blessing or a curse, much as

St. Paul is using the word in this reference from Corinthians: "If you bless with the spirit, how can any one in the position of an outsider say the 'Amen' to your thanksgiving?" (1 Cor 14:16).

In the Old Testament as well, there is a sense that the word was a response from the people, affirming a statement by another speaker in a liturgical fashion as we see in the psalms. As with the word "alleluia," this word has been considered essentially untranslatable, and therefore it has survived the centuries in the scriptures and in the Church's life of prayer as a fundamental affirmation that nothing can cancel or revoke.

In his *Introduction to Christianity*, Benedict attempts to present anew the reasonableness of Faith to those shaped by philosophies of pragmatism, where all things must be measurable by human reason. He looks at the Hebrew in a line from Isaiah: "If you will not believe (*ta' aminu*), surely you shall not be established (*te' amenu*)" (Is 7:9). This is a play on the word "aman" in both clauses, which stems from the same root as amen, and means to build up or support. King Ahaz, in Isaiah, wanted to form an alliance with the Assyrians, but the prophet tells him he will do better if he trusts in God, the support and defender of Israel. Benedict uses this verse to illustrate the distinction between knowing as calculation and knowing as trust, as faith. While calculating reason may build remarkable cities, it is not enough to build a life, especially one that hopes to cross the humanly unbridgeable gulf that is death.

Benedict goes on to explain an insight that has accompanied him throughout his career as a theologian. The opening of human reason to faith is not harmful to reason but actually ennobles it to affirm the higher realities that humanity does not make but which we are invited to bring into our lives in order to be transformed. This transformation by grace must be founded on the truth which is God and his unfailing promises. He writes, "The one root of 'mn (Amen) . . . includes the

meanings truth, firmness, firm ground, ground, and further-
more the meanings loyalty, to trust, entrust oneself. . . . Faith
is thereby defined as taking up a position, as taking a stand
trustfully on the ground of the word of God."[1]

Benedict then notes how a merging of understanding
and standing firm in God (especially in the Greek translation
of 7:9) illuminates the essential relationship between the Faith
and truth. Pope Francis, in his first encyclical, *Lumen Fidei*,
partly authored by Benedict, discusses this same verse from
Isaiah in a similar manner, underscoring the importance of
the truth of Faith precisely because it transcends mere data,
illuminated as it is by an uncreated light that is both the origin and purpose of everything that exists (Jn 1:9). Hence the
formulation of St. Augustine: "Believe, so you may understand."[2] How else could we relate to the infinite One who is
not a blind equation of physics or a law but person?

While in the Greek courtyards philosophers were seeking the Absolute, Moses was speaking with him, receiving his
name and the glow of his presence on his own face (Ex 34:35).
Yahweh's name as "I am who I am" gives him a name beyond
all other gods because, while they are not, he supremely is.

The merging of the God of the philosophers and the God
of scripture, far from tainting the original revelation, conveys
the truth of God's reality: both absolute being, origin of all
that exists, and the love, as Dante put it, that moves the sun
and the stars. Benedict writes, "This God of the philosophers,
whose pure eternity and unchangeability had excluded any
relation with the changeable and transitory, now appeared
to the eye of faith as the god of men, who is not only thought
of all thoughts, the eternal mathematics of the universe, but
also *agape*, the power of creative love."[3] The source of this
Faith, of course, is not a symposium for philosophers but the
paschal mystery. In fact, the Eucharist is the ultimate amen,
the unending celebration of Christ's sacrificial offering to
the Father that has brought us the grace of divine adoption.

When we say "amen," we affirm a reality we do not make, nor one we can undo, however much we try. Amen is the rock, the solid ground of all that exists, and from which all things come. It is both Trinitarian fire and endless self-gift that gives the cosmos being simply out of love. In a real sense, Christ himself is our amen, for he is the rock (1 Cor 10:4), the "yes" to all the promises of God (2 Cor 1:20). We utter our amen through him, and it stands.

Here, in this two-syllable, untranslatable word, *amen*, we find the ground on which we stand and trust in the promises of God.

Our "amen" speaks not so much of an end as of a beginning without end. Pope Francis cites Nietzsche in his encyclical as presenting the charge that Christian faith is the death of seeking, intellectual searching, and the adventure of finding new paths in life. With a single sentence, Francis parries the charge with a truth so obvious no one can deny it: "The light of autonomous reason is not enough to illumine the future" or any other of the magisterial mysteries of life, which need a source more than human for enlightenment and healing.[4]

St. Thomas Aquinas portrays the act of faith in simple terms that nevertheless capture the adventure of belief: "As regards the intellect, the assent of faith is a lowly operation; for the intellect does not see what is believed. But as regards the object of the assent, the operation may be most sublime. ... The desire is not quieted but rather excited by the knowledge of faith, for everyone desires to see what he believes."[5]

This one passage contains, in a real sense, the whole project of theology—faith seeking understanding, yearning for vision. Countless cathedrals, with all their exquisite beauty, have been raised to heaven by this thirst to catch a glimpse of the infinite beauty of God.

Beautiful as such cathedrals are, they nevertheless point to higher realities, at once exalted in eternity and as intimate and as personal as grace when it touches the innermost recesses of our hearts. For this reason, we make our Morning

Offering through the Immaculate Heart of Mary, pure beyond compare with the resplendent beauty of holiness. She is the true tabernacle of the Lord, and we cannot imagine a life of prayer without her most powerful intercession. She will keep our thirst for the vision of her Son faithful and true.

But as we close this reflection on offering our day to the Lord, we might also look for assistance toward someone very close to Our Lady. His life too was an offering, something very like the "salt" spoken of by Jesus in Matthew's gospel, a preservative that protects from the corruptions of self-love that is, in the end, our primary enemy. His quiet life, too, is like the leaven spoken of in the same parable: his humility silently offered all things to God, viewing them in the light of eternity. At the end, he was content to disappear into the endless embrace of God.

I am speaking, of course, of St. Joseph. Pope John Paul II called him the "Guardian of the Redeemer." For centuries, Christians have venerated him as the protector of the Holy Family, master of the interior life. As St. Josemaría Escrivá noted, Jesus must have resembled Joseph in many "features of his character, in his way of speaking . . . his realism, his eye for detail, the way he sat at table and broke bread, his preference for everyday situations to give doctrine—all this reflects his childhood and the influence of Joseph."[6] Citing Christian tradition, and Genesis (41:55), St. Josemaría tells us, "Get to know Joseph and you will find Jesus. Talk to Joseph and you will find Mary, who always sheds peace about her in that attractive workshop in Nazareth."[7]

Today, as never before, we need the protection of St. Joseph. Forces that can only be called demonic have risen up to attack the Faith, the Church, the priesthood, the family, and marriage. St. Joseph was not afraid of the darkness, whether in the chill of night, when a family must be moved with stealth and speed, or in the uncertainty that comes with our human condition in a fallen world. His days on this earth, we should remember, were spent among Roman governors and deranged kings with their own armies.

Pope Benedict XVI, in his volume on the infancy narratives in his trilogy *Jesus of Nazareth*, gives us a glimpse into how this man lived for God in the middle of the world. While discussing Mary's sudden pregnancy, Benedict ponders Joseph's actions as recounted in St. Matthew's gospel. Joseph had betrothed her but also knew he was not the father. Joseph's acceptance of his vocation to be the spouse of Mary, even though she would remain ever-virgin, stems from his rich interior life, always receptive to the divine will, even when he did not understand that will or where it would lead him. Here is Benedict's brief portrait of Joseph:

> This image of the just man with roots in the living waters of God's word, whose life is spent in dialogue with God and who therefore brings forth constant fruit—this image becomes concrete in the event recounted here, as well as in everything we are subsequently told about Joseph of Nazareth. After the discovery that Joseph made, his task was to interpret and apply the law correctly. He does so with love; he does not want to give Mary up to public shame. He wishes her well, even in the hour of his great disappointment. He does not embody the form of externalized legalism that Jesus denounces in Matthew 23 and that Paul opposes strenuously. He lives the law as Gospel.[8]

This is exactly the way we want to live our Morning Offering: with roots deep in the living waters of God's word. We want to offer our prayer, our work, our joys, and our sufferings of this day, as St. Joseph did, with a heart seeking continual purification before God's loving presence. Lived this way, our Morning Offering can be humanly and supernaturally fruitful. St. Joseph, with his unity of life, combines action and contemplation, law and love. His life, however, is not so much a paradigm of balance as it is a faithful response to the grace of God, to that love that is "strong as death" (Sg 8:6).

We should get to know Joseph. He is surely, as with the best of friends, a good listener. This man of profound prayer and trust, who by all accounts did not live to see the great events of Jesus' public life, will show us how to offer our days to the Lord with simplicity.

When Jesus began his ministry, it caused a stir in all of Judea. "Is not this the carpenter's son? Is not his mother called Mary?" (Mt 13:55). No doubt in those early years, there was nothing unusual, in the sense of being different, in that little shop. The clean smell of cut wood, the tools all at hand or neatly in their place, and perhaps a little forge for firing iron into hinges and hooks: that is all. Yet what peace must have reigned in that place! Work done in the presence of the incarnate Word is always prayer.

But when they did stop to pray, as Joseph surely would, a devout Jew from the house of David, we can only wonder at their piety. To pray, Jews in the ancient world would naturally turn toward the Holy City of Jerusalem. That would mean, for Joseph, turning southward. It would only be logical to do so, after Joseph's father and so many before him.

Yet sometimes—in a reverie, perhaps—one can imagine something different, consistent with the newness that had already come into the world, which was, in fact, standing by Joseph's side. Could Joseph have picked up a hint, now and again, of another hope, coming not from Jerusalem but from a descendent of King David who is also David's Lord?

Would Joseph the worker, the master of interior life, have been tempted during morning prayer to turn to this Son, the true Light of the World? From all we know, Jesus would not have given anything away, for his hour had not yet come (Jn 2:4). Perhaps, as a concession, Jesus would have looked eastward, where in due time the rising sun would mark countless renewals of his perfect and acceptable offering, the *liturgia* of his holy Bride, the offering of offerings, whereby we rise to heaven as on Jacob's ladder.

Yet if Joseph turned eastward too and saw in those first hints of dawn an image of unfailing promise, like the first morning, surely the child (who was a child and infinitely more) would have given him at least a smile?

$\mathcal{A}$ Final Offering

And so, Lord, we see in your light the unending "yea-saying" of the first morning of creation, which will not be undone (which can never be undone in an eternity of worlds). For the light that enlightens each one has walked among us (Jn 1:9). Though hatred still can blind our broken but grace-filled world, you bring every turning heart to the Father through the way of self-giving. You show us how each morning we can meet you anew, aided and refashioned by the delicate breath of your Spirit, until the unending day when all be one with you, O Lover of Souls.

$\mathcal{A}$ppendix 1
A Weekly Plan for Living the Morning Offering

By virtue of our Baptism, all Christians are called to holiness of life. This means living out our baptismal promises in the midst of the world and, in the words of Vatican II, "renewing the temporal order." That renewal will only come from supernatural grace. Blessed John Henry Newman put this challenge and opportunity this way: "We attain to heaven by using this world well, though it is to pass away; we perfect our nature, not by undoing it, but by adding to it what is more than nature, and directing it to ends higher than its own."[1]

Newman puts first things first, allowing the light of faith to illuminate this world as good yet fallen, as coming from the hand of God but needing cleansing in the blood of his only Son, Jesus Christ. In this way, the smallest detail of our daily lives can, in the words of Henry David Thoreau, become "lurking places" for the divine.

One way of renewing the temporal order is to use the various days of the week as reminders of the Lord's entrance into history in the person of Jesus. Traditionally, Catholics have set aside each day for a special remembrance of some aspect of the Faith. For instance, Sunday is unique in the endless rounds of weeks and years as it is the Lord's Day, the morning of his resurrection, and the definitive defeat of spiritual death and the opening of the gates of heaven. Thursday is devoted to special attention to the institution of the priesthood and the Eucharist, the latter being the "source and summit" of our lives. Friday, of course, is dedicated to the Lord's Passion and death on the Cross; Saturday, to Our Lady, who waited with undiminished faith for the Lord's return from the gates of the underworld.

The following reflections are intended to help us make a Morning Offering in tune with the riches of our Catholic Faith as evoked by the weekly calendar. It is true that each day of the week is a new day, reborn in grace. Yet that grace, while primarily streaming from God's eternity, also has a historical dimension. When we contemplate both, we find ourselves in the midst of the mystery of the Incarnation, God's embrace of this material, temporal world into his own heart.

Monday

AN INVITATION TO THE HOLY SPIRIT AND INTERCESSION FOR THE SOULS IN PURGATORY

This is a day in which we can make our Morning Offering remembering that we do so in cooperation with the Holy Spirit, the sanctifier of our souls. This devotion helps us avoid the stressful (and false) position of thinking our holiness of life is primarily due to our own efforts. While the moral law is a light leading to the Lord, we are called to something other than—though not less than—moral perfection: union with the triune God for all eternity. Ultimately, we are not the protagonist of our own life but should live in docility to the Spirit of the Lord.

In the early hours of our day, we should confidently invoke the Holy Spirit and ask him for his seven gifts: piety, fear of the Lord, knowledge, wisdom, counsel, fortitude, and understanding. Because the Holy Spirit is a divine person, we can talk with him in our prayer, asking for lights to see our way in this pilgrimage of faith, knowing that "in everything God works for good with those who love him," and resting in his infinite goodness and care for us (Rom 8:28). We walk by faith not sight, but we also have the comforter, the Paraclete, our advocate before the Father, who seals us with his truth and his gentle presence, found not in the whirlwind but in the silence of prayer.

Tuesday

SPECIAL ACKNOWLEDGMENT OF THE HOLY GUARDIAN ANGELS

On this day, we can give special attention to our guardian angel, a minister of God who is tasked from our conception with getting us to heaven and protecting us from evil. We should make our Morning Offering with our guardian angel. He is right by our side at all hours. All the angels of God behold the Father's face in heaven. They are filled with sanctifying grace, the bliss, and the beatitude of the eternal vision of God, and yet they are also with us every step of our journey. We should generally do many if not all of our practices of piety and prayer with our guardian angels—this gives us the correct sense that we are never alone, and their awesome presence will inspire us to a more sincere desire to grow in the moral and theological virtues.

Wednesday

INVOKE THE INTERCESSION OF ST. JOSEPH

We can make our Morning Offering on Wednesday with a view to St. Joseph's quiet virtues and fidelity to his vocation. In his earthly pilgrimage, he was the Virgin Mary's husband and, as St. John Paul II called him, the guardian of the Redeemer.[2] His courage found its origin in his deep interior life. When the call of God came to Joseph, whether in extraordinary fashion or by the events of everyday life, his answer was always prompt and lovingly attentive to the details. Joseph will teach us to work in the presence of the Lord, taking good days as well as bad, and offering them to God with a patience that watches and waits, intent on not show but the reality of divine love hidden in the most ordinary moments of life.

St. Joseph also reminds us that the prelude to the Passion was an interior betrayal, a loss of personal fidelity to little things, and in this way an estrangement from the truth that is the way to God. By offering little, unnoticed sacrifices to God with Joseph's intercession, may we never grow tired of the hidden life of grace that seeks only the Lord.

Thursday

WE ADORE THE BLESSED SACRAMENT

When possible, it may be helpful to attend daily Mass or to pay a visit to Jesus in his eucharistic presence at your parish. When this is not possible, there are many ways we can live our Morning Offering on this day dedicated as it is to the Eucharist. We can make our offering to the Lord praying in a special way for all priests and bishops who through their ministerial priesthood offer the sacrifice of the Mass "through which the work of our redemption is accomplished" each day anew.[3] As well, we can spend some time in adoration before the tabernacle, knowing that Christ is with us in a totally unique way in the Blessed Sacrament.

If we have a chance, we can also attend Benediction at our parish or a local oratory, chanting ancient hymns of praise to the God who is with us. In the intimacy of adoration, we can bring all our day—indeed, our whole life—to Jesus while we converse with him in a language of the heart that is often too deep for words. This kind of prayer is the seed ground of many virtues, many vocations, and many fruits of holiness that will not come in any other way. Time and again, we can see how God will not force the will of anyone. Only in the secret places of the heart does grace do its work, which tends usually to take years of maturation before it begins to blossom with the beauty of holiness. Thursday's Morning Offering can in this way go straight to the heart of the eucharistic Christ, developing the strength of a friendship based on the promises of God.

Friday

WE REMEMBER CHRIST'S PASSION AND HIS SACRED HEART

Catholics since apostolic times have remembered Christ's sufferings and death on the Cross on this day. Since Christianity is not a merely intellectual exercise but a living of the mysteries of Christ's life and death, Fridays have also been days particularly marked out for penance and sacrifice. Some countries still abstain from meat on this day, while others suggest some other form of penance.

While it is true that abstinence is a way to unify and make explicit Catholic identity, this is far from the deepest or most profitable motives for such sacrifices. It is better to follow St. Paul's advice that those who have died with Christ will also rise with him. In fact, Christ's own words about the grain of wheat falling to the ground give us all the motivation we need to take up joyfully the Cross in our lives, realizing that only in the light of Faith does suffering make sense, only in the mystery of Christ does the mystery of human suffering take on meaning and light.

This day of the week is also important because of its connection to the Sacred Heart of Jesus. Many Catholics make a "First Friday's Devotion" in honor of the Sacred Heart and go to Mass and receive Communion in reparation to the Lord for a consecutive nine months. This is an excellent way to live the Morning Offering with its important relationship to the Sacred Heart. By this devotion, we renew our understanding that God loves us with a human heart and desires our heart to beat in union with his own.

Saturday

WE HONOR OUR LADY

One can only imagine the way Mary strengthened the apostles during the day of that first Holy Saturday. Though she had seen the worst that a mother can see—her only son dying in agony—she must have known that in those impossible hours the Lord would triumph. Darkness and sin would not have the last word, for her son or for the world created from the primal goodness of God. So she prayed and hoped with a holy hope that looks only to God. This is how Catholics remember Our Lady on this day, and it is in this hope—a Marian one, purest lily of the world—that we can strive to make our Morning Offering each Saturday.

We join in devotion to the Immaculate Heart of Mary, making, if we wish, a "First Saturday's Devotion" of five first Saturdays in reparation to her Immaculate Heart. Many recognize how the heart is truly alive only when we love. This deeply human reality has been lifted to a divine level in the Incarnation of the Word. God's infinite distance is due to the fact that he is the author of all that is and thus like no other. Yet this "otherness" is revealed to us in Christ as the otherness of an unquenchable love. The heart of Mary is a living icon of God's love for the world, drawn as close to us as a mother's heart. In the night of every Saturday we can see the first light of that dawn that will never end. We make our Morning Offering this day by that light, reflected in the heart and the eyes of our heavenly Mother.

Sunday

WE OFFER OURSELVES TO THE HOLY TRINITY, RECALLING THE RESURRECTION OF THE LORD

The Lord's Day is the new and definitive Sabbath. Here our Morning Offering finds its inspiration, goal, and ultimate rest. The first morning of creation is renewed in a supernatural manner by the rising of Jesus Christ from the dead. He is the Risen One, whom death can touch no more. Every prayer uttered from a sincere heart finds its fulfillment in him. All the scriptures point to this second morning in which the world is reborn in grace.

So we make our Morning Offering every day, though particularly on this day, in the light of the Resurrection. In Christ, the unfathomable riches of the Holy Trinity are revealed to humanity. The entire material world is drawn up into the heart of God. Through a life of faith, lived in the celebration of the sacramental gifts, we too offer all we have and are to the Father, through the Son, and in the Holy Spirit. By the adoption of grace, we make our offerings one with the Beloved One, knowing he will never reject those he gave his life to save.

*A*ppendix 2

Reflection Questions and Observations to Guide Your Reading

Introduction

- Do I begin my day with the Morning Offering? Do I say it prayerfully? Do I let its meaning penetrate my heart?

- Do I ponder the gift of my Baptism, which makes me a child of God? Do I see the sacraments of the Church as God's plan for the renewal of his creation?

- Do I realize the necessity of God's grace in my life? Do I see Jesus as *merely* a moral teacher and forget that he is the Lord of heaven and earth and in this way deserves the adoration of every creature, including me?

- Do I see Holy Mass as the core of all my offerings to God? Do I try to place on the paten of every Mass I attend all the details of my life, adding even my failures so as to better experience God's mercy?

- Do I remember that my heart can be a sanctuary for God, a garden in which the light of the Resurrection shines its warmth? Do I realize that although this intimacy will only fully flower in eternity, it begins this morning, in the hiddenness of grace?

OPPORTUNITIES

- Take a moment before you begin the Morning Offering, and place before you a specific need, a specific concern or worry, and a specific person you know in need of God's grace, and then bring them to your offering.

- Realize you are saying the Morning Offering with millions of other Catholics each day, and your prayer for the intentions of your family and friends and the Holy Father will certainly bear fruit in God's time.

- Meditate on a passage of the gospels in which Jesus prays or speaks about prayer, especially Matthew 5:44, 6:9–13, 14:13, 21:22; Luke 6:12, 9:18, 18:1–14; Mark 9:29; John 17; and Jesus' last words from the Cross in Matthew 27:45–56. Reflect on the offering aspect of each passage.

- Read a passage from St. Thérèse of Lisieux's autobiography, *The Story of a Soul*. Do something little for God with great love, for souls, for conversions, and for mercy for the whole world.

Chapter 1:Jesus

REFLECTIONS

- Do I have a personal relationship with Jesus Christ? Do I realize he created and redeemed not only the world but my very self?

- Do I live the life of Faith with heart, mind, body, and soul? Is my faith perhaps too intellectual? Is it primarily of the heart? Do I pray for the grace to find a healing balance between the two?

- Do I take care of my heart and my body, and realize it is the dwelling place of God?

- Do I put into action the truth that charity is the greatest of the virtues? Do I pray for the help to keep my soul lit with the fire of God's love?

- Do I realize that Jesus is waiting to meet me in the sacrifice of the Mass? And do I know that his redemptive gift on Calvary now comes to me under the humble appearances of bread and wine?

- Do I give time each time to speak with Jesus by the light of the tabernacle candle? Do I adore him there—and at all times?

- Does my Morning Offering take its strength from the Mass, which is the strength of God's love for the world and for me?

OPPORTUNITIES

- Renew your Morning Offering several times a day in union with all the Masses offered today.

- Read a short passage from the gospels each day. Reflect on how Christ shows us the way to the Father, the way of the gift of self that is love.

- When you feel tired or discouraged, offer those feelings to Christ so he may offer them to your Father in heaven and shower you with his graces.

- See in the mysteries of life the greater mysteries of God and his revelation in Christ. By the light of Faith, you can see the world and all things from God's loving point of view.

- When you can't understand an event or a person, reflect on the fact that Christ understands everything completely and is acting even now in your life and the life of the world.

Chapter 2: Immaculate Heart

REFLECTIONS

- Do I realize that the fullness of God's promises has entered the world through Mary? Do I take advantage of this truth in my prayer, developing a tender, filial love for her?

- Do I make small, unnoticed sacrifices and offer them to God through Mary?

- Do I make my Morning Offering with Mary by my side? Do I ask her to help me make my offering sincere?

- Do I realize that Our Lady is fully human, and hence her response to God's graces is a permanent inspiration for me in my daily life?

- Do I take care to remember that God is not interested in artificial saints but in saints that bring all their humanity under the renewal of grace?

OPPORTUNITIES

- When difficulties come your way, offer them to Mary throughout the day. She is full of empathy for she knows how deeply the heart can hurt.

- Pray a decade of the Rosary meditating specifically on Mary's offering of herself to God for the Church and the world.

- Ask Mary to inspire you to some specific acts of charity for those around you, and thank her for this afterward.

- When you say something, be like Our Lady, and let your words come from the silence of your prayer and presence of God.

Chapter 3: Prayers

REFLECTIONS

- Do I realize the all-important place of prayer in my life?

- Do I ask Jesus to teach me to pray, as the apostles prayed? Do I listen in my prayer, or is my prayer mostly a monologue?

- Do I consider prayer a "task" rather than what it truly is: a conversation with God?

- When I pray, do I ask for the grace to enter into the trinitarian mystery as revealed by Christ and his Church?

Opportunities

- Try to set aside specific times for prayer: in the morning, afternoon, and evening. Be flexible but also faithful to this.

- Strive to know the Holy Spirit better by reading the letters of St. Paul, remembering that the Holy Spirit is known as the sanctifier of our souls.

- Read a good book on the liturgy of the Church, and try to grow in the knowledge of this "perfect prayer" of Jesus Christ to the Father.

- Pick a time in the day for mental prayer in which a simple glance of love takes in some fundamental truths of our Faith.

- Spend twenty minutes or so reflecting on the words of the Our Father, thinking about their richness, beauty, and truth about God and ourselves.

Chapter 4: Works

Reflections

- Do I see work as something that contributes to the building up of the world according to God's will for humanity and for me personally?

- Do I offer the difficulties of my work to God for reparation for my soul and for the world?

- Am I conscientious about my work? Do I try to serve God in my work, knowing that one of my main responsibilities is fulfilling the duties of my state in life?

- Do I place on the paten at Mass all my worries about my job? Do I strive to maintain a balance between professional work and family life? Do I realize that work is, ultimately, only a means for me to serve my family, neighbors, and God himself?

OPPORTUNITIES

- Take time to perform some favor for a coworker in a way that isn't noticed.

- Pause in a moment of difficult work, and briefly renew your Morning Offering in a few deeply felt words.

- If a coworker seems upset, ask him or her what is wrong and if you can help.

- Turn your desk at home or work into an altar by offering up an hour of intense work for the intentions of the Holy Father.

Chapter 5: Joys

REFLECTIONS

- Do I take stock of the joys in my life in the light of Christ? Am I deeply convinced that all good comes from God? Do I know that God is my Father and all that happens to me is under his loving providence?

- Is my perspective sufficiently supernatural, viewing all of the events of my life—good and bad—in the light of eternity?

- Do I fail to dig deeper into the reality of life, and do I stay on the surface of things, afraid of the intimacy and challenges of prayer before the Lord?

- Do I realize that no matter how dark the shadows of this life, they will never be able to overcome the light of Easter Morning?

- Do I realize that the deepest wellsprings of joy lie in the interior life? Do I realize that I was created for the joy and bliss of heaven and that the life of grace is a prelude to eternal life?

OPPORTUNITIES

- Make a daily effort to see all things as they are: gifts of God's infinite generosity.

- Take time to savor the simplicities of life—a child's smile, a flower, or a friendship—knowing that their goodness has its source in God.

- Make real this day Christ's words, "It is more blessed to give than to receive" (Acts 20:35). Take joy in the gift of self to God and to others for the love of God.

- At today's Mass, thank the Lord for all his gifts, especially the gift of himself in Holy Communion.

Chapter 6: Sufferings

REFLECTIONS

- Do I see suffering in the light of Faith? Do I realize that such suffering taken with a supernatural spirit purifies me?

- Do I realize that as a creature my perspective is limited, partial, and incomplete? Do I act on this truth by being humble in God's eyes?

- Do I sometimes focus on only the negative? Do I realize that every Mass is a celebration of Christ's victory over sin and death?

- Do I meditate on the goodness of creation that however marred by sin still gives witness to God's glory?

OPPORTUNITIES

- Make a visit to a museum or art gallery, and ponder the amazing gift of being made in the image of God.

- Visit an elderly care house, and see what you can do to help those who have no one to visit them.

- Spend an hour before the Blessed Sacrament praying for those in hospitals or those suffering from mental illness.

Chapter 7: This Day

REFLECTIONS

- Do I give sufficient attention to the way God reveals himself in the natural world? Do I fail to see an image of his providence in the intricate harmonies of the seasons, for instance?

- Do I put my anxieties about the future on the paten of the Mass? Do I realize that Christ's offering is now mine, and so I can rest in the peace of being a child of God, no matter what happens?

- Do I take comfort in knowing that God is a loving Father who cares for his children with infinite wisdom?

- Do I bring the truth of the Faith to my heart by letting it sink in during prayer or the reading of sacred scripture?

OPPORTUNITIES

- Take a walk at a quiet time of the day, and reflect on the goodness of God visible in nature and even in the city-scapes of the world.

- Read some poetry that evokes the wonder of creation. Read some Gerard Manley Hopkins, for instance, and see how a sensitive heart falls in love with God's providential hand seen in nature.

- Immerse yourself in a simple activity, knowing that God dwells within and without, especially in the silence of love.

- Speak to God in the silence of your heart many times during the day, knowing that his hiddenness is an invitation for you to get to know him better.

Chapter 8: Sacred Heart

REFLECTIONS

- Does my spiritual life give enough attention to the Sacred Heart of Jesus? Do I at times neglect prayer and in this way open myself to superficiality?

- Do I realize when I sin I contribute to the wounding of the Sacred Heart of Jesus when he suffered his Passion?

- Do I understand that the Lord wants to give me a new heart, one that is in union with his own?

- Do I realize that this devotion to the Sacred Heart of Jesus has treasures of grace and mercy that our day deeply needs?

OPPORTUNITIES

- Pray the Litany to the Sacred Heart of Jesus, asking in particular for graces of conversion, first for yourself and then for the Church and the world.

- Reflect on a habit that you have acquired, and see whether it conforms to the Heart of Jesus found in the gospels and the writings of the saint.

- Attend Holy Mass on the Feast of the Sacred Heart of Jesus, praying specifically for all priests and bishops.

Chapter 9: Holy Mass

REFLECTIONS

- Do I put the Mass at the high point of my day? Do I pray for graces to assist at Mass more reverently each day?

- Do I make my Morning Offering in view of all the Masses said each day? Do I attend Mass with my Morning Offering in mind? Do I place on the priest's paten all my intentions, worries, work, joys, and sorrows?

- Do I try to deepen my knowledge of the Mass by reading the Catholic *Catechism* and other books of faith to learn how the Church understands the Eucharist?

- Do I foster a sense of active concern for my neighbor, and do I carry the love of Christ to him or her after Mass?

OPPORTUNITIES

- Pray for all priests. Offer to help them in their ministry by prayer and material assistance, if needed.

- Get to Mass as often as you can. Invite friends and family.

- Make the Mass the source and inspiration of your Morning Offering. Your offering will grow in effectiveness and authenticity to the degree that it is eucharistic.

Chapter 10: Thanksgiving

REFLECTIONS

- Do I cultivate a sense a gratitude for the blessings of life? Do I realize that all of the good things in my life find their origin in God? Do I thank him for this?

- Do I make Communions of thanksgivings for the favors I have received from God? Does my Morning Offering express a spirit of thanksgiving?

- Do I realize that true joy is an expression of love?

OPPORTUNITIES

- Stop a few times during the day, and raise your heart in thanksgiving for your life, your family, your work, your joys, and your faith.

- Write someone a note telling them you are grateful he or she is your friend.

- Tell the Lord you always want to have a thankful heart.

Chapter 11: Reparation

REFLECTIONS

- Is my conscience awake to the necessity of reparation for my own sins and the sins of the world? Do I see sin as an abstraction instead of what it is, an offense against God's love?

- Do I seek out freely small, unnoticed acts of sacrifice to make reparation to the Sacred Heart of Christ?

- Do I see the humility of Christ as a motive for fidelity to his will for me?

OPPORTUNITIES

- Offer a Rosary in reparation against a certain grave sin: for instance, abortion, human trafficking, pornography, and so forth.

- Read a book on Christ's sufferings on Cavalry to deepen your sense of his offering of his life on the Cross for us.

Chapter 12: Apostolate

REFLECTIONS

- Do I strive to live a moral life because I am motivated by a love of God and neighbor? Do I realize that love is the perfection of all the virtues? And do I know that love itself is the highest virtue?

- Do I remember that aside from sin being primarily an offense against God's goodness, it also harms my neighbor and fellow Christian?

- Do I live my life with a lively awareness of my responsibility to bring the light of the Gospel wherever I go?

- Do I see my family life as an excellent way to spread the joy of the Gospel to other families?

OPPORTUNITIES

- Try to make time for your family in a way that is natural and unrushed, spending time together. Invite other families over for lunch after Mass, for instance, to get to know each other better.

- Make sure your Morning Offering is done with a sense of apostolic zeal. How we begin our day affects our own families and many others.

- Begin each day with a few friends in mind when making your Morning Offering, asking God throughout the day to bless them.

Chapter 13: The Holy Father

REFLECTIONS

- Do I sometimes have too narrow a view of the Church? Do I concentrate simply on the human dimension of the Church's life, forgetting it is a divinely founded institution?

- Do I understand that authority is something that can and should be put at all times in the service of love?

- Do I remember that the Church is essentially a mystery of faith and must be believed and loved in this way?

- Do I see my Morning Offering as an effective and important way to help the Holy Father? Do I realize I can renew this intention many times a day?

OPPORTUNITIES

- Read a papal document or speech found at Vatican.va, and bring it to your prayer for the pope's intentions.

- Ask Our Lady this morning to help the pope in a particular way to carry the burdens of his office and govern the Church with supernatural wisdom.

- Say the Angelus at noon today for the pope's intentions.

Chapter 14: Amen

REFLECTIONS

- Do I take strength from the certainty of the Faith when I make my Morning Offering?

- Do I renew my Morning Offering a few times during the day?

- Do I desire to deepen my faith by prayer, sacrament, and spiritual reading?

- Do I really try to get to know Our Lady and St. Joseph? Do I realize they can teach me a lot about Jesus and how I can be a better disciple of the Lord?

OPPORTUNITIES

- Reflect on the word "amen," meditating on how it expresses how your faith is anchored in the reality of God.

- Practice silence for some time each day. Speak to God in this silence, and listen to his responses.

- Read the infancy narrative in St. Luke's gospel. Let the mystery of God's humility inspire your Morning Offering.

otes

Introduction

1. Yusuf Cat Stevens, "Quotes: A Few Good Songs," accessed September 15, 2014, http://www.yusufislam.com.

2. Alexander Solzhenitsyn, "Nobel Lecture," Nobelprize.org, 1970, accessed August 5, 2014, http://www.nobelprize.org.

3. Frances Claire Sayers, "Eleanor Farjeon's 'Room with a View,'" *Horn Book* 32, no. 5 (1956), accessed August 17, 2014, http://www.eldrbarry.net.

4. Benedict XVI, "St. Augustine's Last Days, 'Though the World Grows Old, Christ Is Forever Young,'" General Audience, January 16, 2008, accessed August 1, 2014, http://www.pierced-hearts.org.

5. Robert P. Moncreiff, *Bart Giamatti: A Profile* (New Haven, CT: Yale University Press, 2007), 50.

6. Thomas Aquinas, *Summa Theologiae*, vol. 4, 3.1.1 (Allen, TX: Christian Classics, 1981), 2019 (emphasis added).

7. Alexander Schmemann, *For the Life of the World* (Crestwood, NY: St. Vladimir's Seminary Press, 1973), 14–15.

8. William Shakespeare, *The Merchant of Venice*, in *The Riverside Shakespeare*, ed. G. Blakemore Evans and J. J. M. Tobin, 2nd ed. (Boston: Houghton Mifflin, 1996), 314, v. 1.58–61.

9. Adin Steinsaltz, *A Guide to Jewish Prayer* (New York: Schocken Books, 2000), 49.

10. *The Month: A Catholic Magazine and Review*, Vol. 65, January to April, 1889, (London: Burns & Oates), 396–406.

11. Henri Ramiere, *The Apostleship of Prayer* (Philadelphia: Messenger of the Sacred Heart, 1889), viii.

12. "Saint Therese of Lisieux—Popular Catholic Saint," Catholic-Saints-Resource-Center.com, accessed August 5, 2014, http://www.catholic-saints-resource-center.com.

13. John Paul II, World Congress of National Secretaries of the Apostleship of Prayer, April 13, 1985, http://www.ewtn.com.

14. "Propositions of Synod on the Eucharist, Nos. 41–45," November 4, 2005, accessed August 17, 2014, http://www.zenit.org, proposition 43.

1. Jesus

1. John Henry Newman, "Sermon 10: Faith and Reason, Contrasted as Habits of Mind," Newman Reader: Works of John Henry Newman, accessed August 5, 2014, http://www.newmanreader.org.

2. Jean-Baptiste Chautard, *The Soul of the Apostolate* (Charlotte, NC: TAN Books, 1977), 26.

3. Roch A. Kereszty and O. Cist, *Jesus Christ: Fundamentals of Christology* (New York: Alba House, 2011), 46.

4. Aquinas, *Summa Theologiae*, vol. 1, 1.1.8, 5–6.

5. Kereszty and Cist, *Jesus Christ*, 3.

6. "Czeslaw Milosz with Helen Vendler, 26 March 1998," accessed August 17, 2014, http://www.youtube.com.

7. Benedict XVI, *Joseph Ratzinger in Communio*, vol. 2, *Anthropology and Culture* (Grand Rapids, MI: Eerdmans, 2013), 92.

8. Ibid., 97.

9. Paul VI, *Gaudium et Spes* 22, Holy See, promulgated December 7, 1965, accessed August 5, 2014, http://www.vatican.va.

10. "Preface II of the Ascension of the Lord," in *Roman Missal* (Collegeville, MN: Liturgical Press, 2008), 570.

11. Avery Dulles, *John Henry Newman* (New York: Bloomsbury Academic, 2009), 324.

2. Immaculate Heart

1. Paul VI, *Lumen Gentium* 64, Holy See, promulgated November 21, 1964, accessed August 6, 2014, http://www.vatican.va.

2. Stephano M. Manelli, *All Generations Shall Call Me Blessed: Biblical Mariology*, rev. and enlarged 2nd ed. (New Bedford, MA: Academy of the Immaculate, 2012), 66.

3. Fulton J. Sheen, *Life of Christ* (New York: Image, 1977), 35.

4. Marie Bernard-Said, trans., *Bernard of Clairvaux: Homilies in Praise of the Blessed Virgin Mary* (Kalamazoo, MI: Cistercian Publications, 1993), 15.

5. Joseph Ratzinger, *The Spirit of the Liturgy* (San Francisco: Ignatius Press, 2000), 140.

6. Josemaría Escrivá, *The Way: The Essential Classic of Opus Dei's Founder* (New York: Image, 1982), 513.

7. Benedict XVI, "Address to 'Scholae Canotorum' Pilgrims," accessed August 18, 2014, http://www.zenit.org.

3. Prayers

1. *The Aquinas Prayer Book: The Prayers and Hymns of St. Thomas Aquinas*, translated by Robert Anderson and Johann Moser (Manchester, NH: Sophia Institute Press, 1993, 2000), 2.

2. Christopher A. Hall, *Worshiping with the Fathers* (Downers Grove, IL: InterVarsity Press, 2009), 198.

3. Columba Marmion, *Christ: The Life of the Soul* (Bethesda, MD: Zaccheus Press, 2005), 44.

4. Escrivá, *The Way*, 513.

5. Benedict Baur, *In Silence with God*, trans. Henry Regnery Company (New Rochelle, NY: Scepter Publishers, 1997), 144–45.

4. Works

1. G. K. Chesterton, *The Everlasting Man* (San Francisco: Ignatius Press, 1993), 173.

2. Thomas E. Woods, *How the Catholic Church Built Western Civilization* (Washington, DC: Regnery Publishing, 2005), 28.

3. Jose Luis Illanes, *The Sanctification of Work* (New Rochelle, NY: Scepter Publishers, 2003), 15.

4. Josemaría Escrivá, *Christ Is Passing By* (New Rochelle, NY: Scepter Publishers, 1974), 2.

5. Andres Vazquez de Prada, *The Founder of Opus Dei: The Life of Josemaría Escrivá*, vol. I, *The Early Years* (New York: Scepter Publishers, 2007), 255.

6. Escrivá, *Christ Is Passing By*, 50.

7. Ibid., 113.

8. Josemaría Escrivá, *Friends of God* (New Rochelle, NY: Scepter Publishers, 2010), 65.

9. Wendell Berry, *Leavings* (Berkeley, CA: Counterpoint, 2010), 3.

5. Joys

1. Benedict XVI, *Deus Caritas Est* 3, Holy See, December 25, 2005, accessed August 7, 2014, http://www.vatican.va.

2. G. K. Chesterton, *The Collected Works of G. K. Chesterton*, vol. 1 (San Francisco: Ignatius Press, 1986), 233.

3. Thomas Aquinas, *Saint Thomas Aquinas: Philosophical Texts*, selected and trans. Thomas Gilby (New York: Oxford University Press, 1960), 275.

4. Joseph Ratzinger, *Jesus of Nazareth: From the Baptism in the Jordan to the Transfiguration* (New York: Doubleday, 2007), 93.

5. Francis de Sales, *Treatise on the Love of God* (Radford, VA: Wilder Publications, 2011), 33.

6. Escrivá, *Christ Is Passing By*, 102.

6. Sufferings

1. Aquinas, *Saint Thomas Aquinas*, 163.

2. John Milton, *Paradise Lost* (Indianapolis: Bobbs-Merrill, 1977), 396.

3. Thomas G. Weinandy, "Does God Suffer?" *First Things*, November 2001, accessed August 8, 2014, http://www.firstthings.com.

4. Ratzinger, *Jesus of Nazareth*, 18.

5. Augustine, *The City of God* (Garden City, NY: Image Books, 1958), 522.

6. Ibid., 522.

7. Ibid., 526.

8. Ibid., 527.

9. Ibid.

10. Ibid., 528.

11. Ibid.

12. Ibid.

13. Ibid.

14. Ibid., 524.

15. *The Catholic Encyclopedia* (New York: Encyclopedia Press, 1913), 255.

7. This Day

1. "In Brief: Fact Sheet; Facts on Induced Abortion Worldwide," Guttmacher Institute, January 2012, accessed August 20, 2014, http://www.guttmacher.org.

2. Roger Clegg, "The Corner: Latest Statistics on Out-of-Wedlock Birth," *National Review Online*, October 11, 2013, accessed August 20, 2014, http://www.nationalreview.com.

3. Francis de Sales, *Introduction to the Devout Life* (New York: Vintage, 2002), 251.

4. Frances de Sales and Pere Huget, *Consoling Thoughts of St. Francis de Sales on God and Providence* (New York: TAN Books, 2013), 77.

5. Jean-Pierre de Caussade, *Abandonment to Divine Providence* (London: Catholic Way Publishing, 2012), 45.

6. Ibid.

7. Ibid., 5.

8. Ibid., 17.

9. Ibid., 16.

10. Ibid., 61.

11. Aquinas, *Summa Theologiae*, I.I.12.6.

12. Caussade, *Abandonment to Divine Providence*, 9.

13. Ibid.

14. Ibid., 5.

15. Ibid., 77.

16. Thomas Aquinas, *Light of Faith: The Compendium of Theology* (Manchester, NH: Sophia Institute Press, 1993), 150–51.

17. Charles Péguy, "The Mystery of the Holy Innocents," Catholic Information Network, accessed August 20, 2014, http://www.centropeguy.org.

8. Sacred Heart

1. Joseph Ratzinger, *Behold the Pierced One* (San Francisco: Ignatius Press, 1986), 54–55.

2. Athanasius, *Ad Serap* I.28.

3. "Letter of Pope Leo the Great to Flavian, Bishop of Constantinople, about Eutyches, 449," in "Tome of Leo," *EWTN*, accessed August 21, 2014, https://www.ewtn.com.

4. Bonaventure, *Opusculum* 3, *Lignum vitae*, 29–30; 47: *Opera omnia* 8, 79.

5. Margaret Mary Alacoque, *The Autobiography of St. Margaret Mary Alacoque* (Charlotte, NC: TAN Books, 2012), 94.

6. Ibid., 95.

7. Ibid., 81.

8. Ratzinger, *Behold the Pierced One*, 59–60.

9. Holy Mass

1. John Paul II, *Ecclesia de Eucharista* 25, Holy See, April 17, 2003, accessed August 11, 2014, http://www.vatican.va.

2. Ignatius of Antioch, "Letter to the Ephesians" 20, *New Advent*, accessed August 21, 2014, http://www.newadvent.org/fathers/0104.htm.

3. Irenaeus, *Adv. haer.* 4.18.5; SC 100 610, *The Ante-Nicene Fathers*, vol. 1 (Hendrickson Publishers, 1994), 486.

4. Ambrose, *Letters 1–91*, trans. Mary Melchior Beyenka (Washington, DC: Catholic University of America Press, 2001), 236.

5. Vonier, *A Key to the Doctrine of the Eucharist* (Bethesda, MD: Zaccheus Press, 2003), 107.

6. Lambert Beauduin, *Liturgy: The Life of the Church* (Farnborough, UK: Saint Michael's Abbey Press, 2002), 15–16.

7. John Paul II, *Reconciliatio et Paenitentia* (Boston: Daughters of St. Paul, 1985), 8.

8. Marmion, *Christ*, 322.

9. Karl Stehlin, *The Immaculata Our Ideal: The Spirit of the Militia Immaculatae according to Fr. Maximilian Kolbe* (Warsaw: Te Deum, 2005), 69.

10. Escrivá, *The Way*, 678.

11. Gerard Manley Hopkins, *Poems of Gerard Manley Hopkins* (New York: Oxford University Press, 1970), 211.

12. Josef Pieper, *Only the Lover Sings: Art and Contemplation* (San Francisco: Ignatius Press, 1990), 22.

13. Everett Diederich, "Eucharistic Worship outside Mass," in *The New Dictionary of Sacramental Worship*, ed. Peter Fink (Collegeville, MN: Liturgical Press, 1990), 459.

14. Aquinas, *Light of Faith*, 4.

15. Joseph Ratzinger, *The Essential Pope Benedict XVI: His Central Writings and Speeches*, ed. John F. Thornton and Susan B. Varenne (San Francisco: HarperSanFrancisco, 2007), 167–68.

16. John Chrysostom, "Homily 50 on Matthew," New Advent, accessed August 22, 2014, http://www.newadvent.org.

17. George Angus, "The 'Revival' of the Archbishopric of St. Andrews," *Tablet*, October 23, 1886, accessed August 22, 2014, http://archive.thetablet.co.uk.

18. "Damien the Leper," EWTN, 1974, accessed August 22, 2014, http://www.ewtn.com.

19. Francis, "Chrism Mass: Homily of Pope Francis," Holy See, March 28, 2013, accessed August 22, 2014, http://w2.vatican.va.

10. Thanksgiving

1. Dietrich von Hildebrand, "The Case for the Latin Mass," *Triumph* (October 1966), accessed August 11, 2014, http://www.catholic-pages.com.

2. Étienne Gilson, *The Spirit of Medieval Philosophy* (Notre Dame, IN: University of Notre Dame Press, 1991), 127.

3. G. K. Chesterton, *Chaucer* (London: Faber and Faber, 1962), 37.

4. Diederich, "Eucharistic Worship," 459.

5. Jacques Philippe, *In the School of the Holy Spirit* (New York: Scepter Publishers, 2007), 28.

6. Aquinas, *Summa Theologiae*, vol. 3, II.II.20, 1256.

7. James Socias, *Handbook of Prayers, including New Revised Order of Mass* (Downers Grove, IL: Midwest Theological Forum, 2012), 251–52.

8. Berry, *Leavings*, 72–73.

11. Reparation

1. Pius XI, *Miserentissimus Redemptor*, Holy See, May 8, 1928, accessed August 13, 2014, http://www.vatican.va.

2. John Paul II, *Reconciliatio et Paenitentia*, 11.

3. Augustine, *Tractate* 124 (Jn 21:19–25), no. 5, New Advent, accessed August 13, 2014, http://www.newadvent.org.

4. Thomas Aquinas, *Commentary on Aristotle's De Anima*, trans. Kenelm Foster, (South Bend, IN: Dumb Ox Books, 1994), 431.b21.

5. Paul J. Griffiths, *Intellectual Appetite* (Washington, DC: Catholic University of America Press, 2009), 45–46.

6. Augustine, *Tractate* 26 (Jn 6:41–59), no. 5, New Advent, accessed August 13, 2014, http://www.newadvent.org.

7. Pius XI, *Miserentissimus Redemptor*.

8. Aquinas, *Summa Theologiae*, vol. 4, III.48.4, 2279–80.

9. Vonier, *Key to the Doctrine*, 27.

12. Apostolate

1. Mahatma Gandhi, *Collected Works of Mahatma Gandhi*, vol. 64 (New Delhi, India: Publications Division, Ministry of Information and Broadcasting, Government of India, 1994), 202–4.

2. Max Picard, *The World of Silence* (South Bend, IN: Regnery / Gateway, 1952), 32.

3. Josemaría Escrivá, *Conversations with Monsignor Escrivá* (Manila, Philippines: Sinag-Tala Publishers, 1985), 78.

4. Paul VI, *Apostolicam Actuositatem* 2, Holy See, November 18, 1965, accessed August 13, 2014, http://www.vatican.va.

5. Benedict XVI, *Deus Caritas Est* 1.

6. Chautard, *Soul of the Apostolate*, 31.

7. Ibid., 37.

8. G. K. Chesterton, *The Superstition of Divorce* (London: Chatto & Windus, 1920), 61.

9. Thérèse de Lisieux, *Story of a Soul: The Autobiography of St. Thérèse of Lisieux*, 3rd ed. (Washington, DC: ICS Publications, 1996), 201.

13. The Holy Father

1. Ignatius, "To the Romans," trans. Cyril Richardson, Silouan, accessed August 23, 2014, http://silouanthompson.net.

2. Clement of Alexandria, "Who Is the Rich Man that Shall Be Saved?" 21, New Advent, accessed August 13, 2014, http://www.newadvent.org.

3. Optatus, *The Works of St. Optatus, Bishop of Milevis, against the Donatists* (London: Longmans, Green, 1917), 66.

4. John Henry Newman, *An Essay on the Development of Christian Doctrine* (Notre Dame, IN: University of Notre Dame Press, 1989), 1845.

5. George Weigel, *Letters to a Young Catholic* (New York: Basic Books, 2004), 26, 27.

6. Ian Ker, *John Henry Newman* (New York: Oxford University Press, 1988, 2009), 654–56.

7. *Dogmatic Canons and Decrees* (Rockford, IL: Tan Books, 1977), 256.

8. John Henry Newman, *Dr. John Henry Newman's Reply to Mr. Gladstone's Pamphlet* (Toronto: A. S. Irving, 1875), 79.

9. Paul VI, *Lumen Gentium*, 18.

10. Charles Journet, *The Theology of the Church* (San Francisco: Ignatius Press, 2004), 157.

11. G. K. Chesterton, *Heretics* (London: John Lane Company, 1905), 67.

12. Benedict XVI, "Homily of His Holiness Benedict XVI," Holy See, December 8, 2005, accessed August 13, 2014, http://www.vatican.va.

14. Amen

1. Joseph Ratzinger, *Introduction to Christianity* (San Francisco: Ignatius Press, 2004), 40.

2. Augustine, *Tractate* 29 (Jn 7:14–18), New Advent, accessed August 23, 2014, http://www.newadvent.org.

3. Ratzinger, *Introduction to Christianity*, 99.

4. Francis, *Lumen Fidei*, Holy See, June 29, 2013, accessed August 14, 2014, http://w2.vatican.va.

5. Aquinas, *Saint Thomas Aquinas*, 320–21.

6. Escrivá, *Christ Is Passing By*, 120.

7. Ibid., 121.

8. Ratzinger, *Jesus of Nazareth*, 40–41.

Appendix 1: A Weekly Plan for Living the Morning Offering

1. John Henry Newman, *The Idea of a University* (Notre Dame, IN: University of Notre Dame Press, 1986), 93.

2. John Paul II, *Redemptoris Custos*, Holy See, August 15, 1989, accessed August 28, 2014, http://www.vatican.va.

3. Paul VI, *Sacrosanctum Concilium*, Holy See, promulgated December 4, 1963, accessed August 28, 2014, http://www.vatican.va.

Michael J. Ortiz teaches religion and English at The Heights School in Potomac, Maryland, where he has taught for thirty years. He has a bachelor's degree in English from St. Anselm College, and a master's degree in English from Georgetown University.

Ortiz has received three grants from the National Endowment for the Humanities, one of which was an independent fellowship.

The Massachusetts native is the author of *Swan Town: The Secret Journal of Susanna Shakespeare*. Ortiz and his wife, Kathleen, have four children. They live in Washington, DC.

AVE

AVE MARIA PRESS

Founded in 1865, Ave Maria Press,
a ministry of the Congregation of
Holy Cross, is a Catholic publishing
company that serves the spiritual and
formative needs of the Church and its
schools, institutions, and ministers;
Christian individuals and families; and
others seeking spiritual nourishment.

For a complete listing of titles from

Ave Maria Press

Sorin Books

Forest of Peace

Christian Classics

visit www.avemariapress.com

AVE AVE MARIA PRESS
       Notre Dame, IN
A Ministry of the United States Province of Holy Cross